Using Activity Based Management for
Continuous Improvement

by Tom Pryor
Julie Sahm

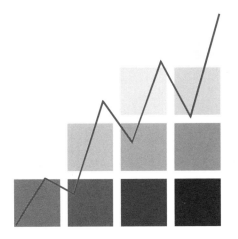

Published by: **ICMS, Inc.**
2261 Brookhollow Plaza
Suite 104
Arlington, Texas 76006
Phone (817) 633-2873
Internet: ICMSABM@aol.com
Web Page: www.ICMS.net

Table of Contents

How to Use This Book..i
  Objective of this book...i
  How to use this book for the first time i
  How to use this book every week ii

Facing a New World of Excellence 1
  Traditional Management 2
  Excellence.. 4
  Activity Based Management (ABM) 7
  Rate your Readiness for Continuous Improvement 8
  Chapter Summary 10

Activity Based Management 13
  Function 14
  Department/Cost Center 14
  Business Process 14
  Activity... 15
  Task 15
  Input 17
  Output 17
  Output Measures 17
  Activity Characteristics 18
  Activity Dictionary 19
  Creating an ABM Information System 20
  Activity Analysis 20
  Activity Analysis Interview 22
  Activity Accounting 24
  Chapter Summary 30

Continuous Improvement Process 33
  Jack's Visit to the Idea Doctor.. 33
  Five Steps to Continuous Improvement 34
  Activity Improvement.. 37
  Process Improvement 38
  Continuous Improvement Teams 41
  ABM Coach 42
  Continuous Improvement Team Meeting 43
  Chapter Summary 46

Table of Contents

Step 1: Identify Improvement Opportunities **49**

   Identify Improvement Opportunities **51**
      Target *51*
      Timeframe *52*
      Training *53*

   Value Analysis **55**
      What is Value Added? *56*
      What is Non-Value Added? *57*
      What do You do with Waste? *58*
      Helpful Hints *61*

   Primary Analysis **63**
      What is Primary? *63*
      What is Secondary? *63*

   Business Process Analysis **69**
      Five Steps to Business Process Analysis *70*

   Benchmarking **79**
      Four Steps to Benchmarking *80*
      Actual Benchmarks *86*
      Helpful Hints *87*

Step 2: Identify Root Cause **91**

   Root Cause Analysis **93**
      Four Steps to Cause-and-Effect Diagrams *94*
      Root Cause Shortcut *98*
      Chapter Summary *100*

Step 3: Identify Possible Solutions **103**

   Brainstorming **105**
      Three Steps to Brainstorming *106*

   Storyboarding **111**
      Five Steps to Storyboarding *112*
      Helpful Hints *114*

Step 4: Implement Best Solution 117

   Developing a Continuous Improvement Plan 119

      Four Steps to Implementing a C.I. Plan 120

      Solution Rating Matrix 121

      Chapter Summary 125

Step 5: Monitor the Improvement 127

   Performance Measurement 129

      Three Principals of Performance Measurement 131

      Activity & Process Performance Measures 132

      Activity Performance Measures 132

      Business Process Performance Measures 140

      Chapter Summary 146

   Activity Based Budgeting 149

      Five Steps to Activity Based Budgeting 150

      Chapter Summary 156

Appendix A: Activity Improvement Example 159

Appendix B: Process Improvement Example 173

Appendix C: Process Improvement Example 183

Index 191

Table of Contents

Team Exercises

Facing a New World of Excellence
Traditional Management Accounting Exercise 3
Activity Based Management Exercise 6

Activity Based Management
What are Your Department's Activities? 27

Value Analysis
Value & Non-Value Definitions 56
Value & Non-Value Classifications 59

Primary Analysis
Primary & Secondary Classification 65

Business Process Analysis
Business Process Exercise 76

Benchmarking
Benchmarking Exercise 86
Improvement Targets 89

Root Cause Analysis
Create a Cause-and-Effect Diagram 97
Do a "Five Why's" Analysis 99

Benchmarking
Brainstorming Exercise 108

Storyboarding
Storyboarding Exercise 114

Developing a Continuous Improvement Plan
Addressing Implementation Problems 124

Performance Measurement
Performance Measures Exercise 130

Activity Based Budgeting
Addressing the Current Budget Process 155

Objective of this book

According to an Institute of Management Accountants' survey each of the last three years, less than 20% of organizations that have implemented Activity Based Management (ABM) or Activity Based Costing (ABC) can point to dollar savings. While there are many reasons for this low success rate, we believe a significant root cause is addressed by this book. All too many organizations have successfully created activity accounting data but lack instruction on how to use the findings to achieve results.

The primary intent of this book is to show each and every person in an organization how to use ABM information combined with the traditional Five Step Continuous Improvement problem-solving process. This combination, augmented with the existing experience of your organization's employees, should result in action programs that move your company closer to cost, time and quality Excellence.

The objective of this book is to explain to every employee how to create, analyze, improve, and measure their department's activity information. A combination of text, graphics, group exercises, team meeting agendas, tips, and detailed examples are provided throughout the sections and Appendices. It is our intent and hope that you will utilize this book as a weekly reference tool to guide your unending journey of continuous improvement.

How to use this book for the first time

Read Chapter One upon receipt of the book. Meet with the other members of your department (or Process Improvement team if you have one) and do the team exercises (noted with a Stop Sign throughout the book). Discuss the results. Be sure to fill out the *Rate Your Readiness for Continuous Improvement* questionnaire in the *Facing a New World of Excellence* chapter. Show and discuss the results with your department manager, process improvement team

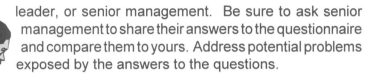

leader, or senior management. Be sure to ask senior management to share their answers to the questionnaire and compare them to yours. Address potential problems exposed by the answers to the questions.

Read the chapter on *Activity Based Management* if you are not familiar with the terminology. Familiarize yourself with the terms, definitions, and examples. If your organization has implemented ABM, have someone give you the reports for your department to review. If your organization does not have ABM in place, use the Activity Based Management section o f this book to guide your implementation of activity analysis and activity accounting. Meet with the members of your department or process improvement team to do and discuss the chapter's team exercises.

Read the *Continuous Improvement* chapter to get a first time overview of how this book combines the proven Five Step problem solving technique with ABM information to support continuous improvement. Do the team exercises.

How to use this book every week

Continuous improvement, as the name implies, is an unending process. Use and refer to the instructions, ideas, and examples throughout the book and Appendices in your weeekly or bi-weekly continuous improvement team meetings. Modify where necessary the recommended meeting agendas, report formats and performance measures to match your own organization's procedures and culture. Mark those changes in your book for ongoing reference.

Celebrate after you and your team members successfully implement a continuous improvement action plan. But remember: When you are done, it is time to return to Step One and begin the process once again.

Facing a New World of Excellence

Motorola has achieved six Sigma quality... 3.2 defects per 1,000,000 products shipped. Wal-Mart collects and reports daily for each of its supplies how much of each product was sold by store, by size and by color... suppliers do not receive paper purchase orders. They receive the order daily electronically. Southwest Airlines can turn around arriving aircraft in 15 minutes... but in an effort to continually improve, they sent a group of employees to interview a Roger Penske Indy 500 pit crew to learn how they do turnarounds in 15 seconds. Striving for Excellence is a part of the culture of those organizations. How about yours?

Facing a New World of Excellence

In today's global market, Continuous Improvement is an absolute necessity. Organizations that do not provide high quality products or services will not survive. Only low cost producers of product and service truly have control of their market. . Products do not last as long due to new technologies, competitors looking for a way to win the customer, and ever changing likes and dislikes of customers. The cumulative impact of these changes is squeezing vital profit margins. Your competition is no longer down the street. They are likely to be on the other side of the world.

You are in a worldwide Continuous Improvement race with competitors you cannot see.

Through all these changes, management and employees are striving to be Excellent. You might be asking yourself, "Hasn't management always tried to be Excellent? If so, then what is different today?" The answer to these questions lies in a management information system that was developed over a century ago.

Traditional management systems promote reasonable goals and reasonable improvement. In the 1970's the Japanese introduced excellence goals... zero defects, zero inventory and zero setup time... and as a result, they made significant improvement. While you may laugh at the thought of excellence actually being achievable, one only need look at the *Wall Street Journal*, *Business Week*, or *Fortune* to read of this week's breakthroughs. Traditional management must be replaced. We are functioning in a different world than 20 years ago.

We are working hard. We are not necessarily working smart!

Most employees feel like they are drowning in a "sea of three-letter quick fixes." How many acronyms can you name?

Traditional Management

Traditional management systems break an organization into functional units of specialists, with a manager assigned to each department or cost center. Each manager is given a budget and is held responsible for staying within the budget guidelines. Proponents of traditional theory believe that if revenue goals are achieved and budget variances are minimized, the organization will be profitable.

What is the shortcoming of Traditional Management? All well-managed companies are busy. They are not, however, busy doing the "right" things which produce value that lead to Excellence. Traditional management information systems focus on managing cost, and not the work that consumes the cost. Traditional Management systems look for "easy fixes" to problems.

Problem	Traditional "Fix"
Sales below plan	Cut spending for discretionary costs such as training and travel.
Sales shrinking	Increase revenue by reducing sales price.
Too many employees	Offer early retirement.
Profits too low	Everyone cut their budget by 10%

Do any of these problems sound familiar? How many fixes has your company implemented? These approaches may lead a company to short term cash improvements, but in the long run they only hurt the company's longevity. *The only way a company can be competitive is to go back to the basics - do the right things, and do them better than the competition. To continually grow and remain a stable organization, a company must truly be Excellent.*

TRADITIONAL MANAGEMENT ACCOUNTING

Team Exercise:

The information presented below depicts traditional management information. Develop three ideas to improve productivity by 10%, assuming sales next year are not going to increase. Is this difficult or frustrating?

RECEIVING DEPARTMENT

Salaries	$545,000
Supplies	88,000
Depreciation	186,000
Space	51,000
All Other	74,000
Total Cost	$944,000

Ideas

1. _____

2. _____

3. _____

Five Principles of Excellence

1. **Continually Manage Activities, not Resources**

2. **Continually Synchronize Activities within Business Processes**

3. **Continually Eliminate Wasteful Activities**

4. **Continually Improve Activity Cost, Time and Quality**

5. **Continually Empower Employees to Improve Activities**

Excellence...

The Honda plant in Ohio ships 400,000 cars per year. When asked how he could operate with a staff of 30 people, the VP of Accounting responded, "You don't have to account for a well designed product going through a well designed process."

Excellence

There are five principles that support the pursuit of Excellence. The first principle is to **Manage Activities, Not Resources.** Focus on what an organization does (an Activity), the cost of doing it, how much work is done, how well the work is done, and how long it takes to complete. By understanding what an organization does, one can begin to challenge whether the organization is doing the right thing. Is it wasteful? Is there a customer or external requirement? Is it the right level of service? Are we doing it efficiently? As exhibited in the previous Receiving Department exercise, the ideas to improve productivity solely by reducing costs is difficult and frustrating. We will repeat the exercise later in this chapter using Activity information.

The second principle of Excellence is to **Synchronize Activities Within Business Processes**. Activities are typically the responsibility of a department or cost center. Yet, an activity is also part of a larger, interdepartmental business process. Optimizing the performance of a function is important. Optimizing the performance of a business process, however, provides greater opportunity to achieve Excellence. We may be organized vertically, but we function horizontally on a daily basis. As *Fortune* magazine described recently, "We will see fewer people with the title 'VP of Sales' by the year 2000 and more people with the title 'VP of Getting Product to the Customers'."

The third principle of Excellence is to **Continually Eliminate Wasteful Activities**. Every organization has some form of waste or non-value added activities. Unfortunately, the cost of waste is hidden in the Traditional Management approach. Employees need an information system that will provide insight into the amount of time spent reworking, expediting, waiting, and inspecting. Most companies find approximately 20% to 30% of their resources are spent performing non-value added activities.

The fourth principle of Excellence is to **Continually Improve Activity Costs, Quality, and Response Time**. Anyone who chooses to rest will likely get run over in the real world of global competition. Do not focus exclusively on the cost of the activity as the sole measure of performance. Producing a product low in cost but poor in quality, and slow to deliver, provides no competitive advantage. Customers want all three: low cost, high quality and quick response. The real challenge is to perform an activity at the lowest cost, highest quality and in the shortest time. To visualize this requirement, consider a 3 legged stool. Have you ever tried to sit on a 3 legged stool when the legs are not even? Imagine the three legs as cost, time and quality. By placing greater emphasis on any one of the legs, a company can jeopardize its success and "fall" out of favor with the customer.

The last principle of Excellence is to **Empower Employees to Continually Improve Their Activities and Processes**. Employee empowerment is not simply pushing decision making to the lowest levels of an organization. Employees must be empowered with information they can understand and act upon **and** supported by a management team that is truly willing to change how the organization goes about its business. Most companies have implemented a slew of three letter acronyms; TQM, JIT, CIM, BPR, but most have failed miserably. On average, only 20% of the companies who have attempted Total Quality Management, Just-In-Time, Computer Integrated Manufacturing or Business Process Re-Engineering have successfully achieved results and sustained the benefits.

If Excellence is to be your goal, your organization must (1) implement an information system based on Activities that empowers everyone to achieve Excellence; (2) senior management commit resources to achieve excellence; and (3) create a culture conducive to Excellence. Some fundamental issues that are essential to this culture:

- **Encourage innovation** - do not penalize mistakes, instead penalize the repetition of mistakes;

- **Provide a performance and reward system** that encourages continuous improvement;

- **Encourage process improvement** rather than merely meeting departmental performance goals;

- Recognize that **Excellence requires many continuous improvement tools.**

Continuous improvement must be measured. Measure the performance of activity costs, quality and time. Do not focus exclusively on cost as the sole measure of continuous improvement. Excessively emphasizing one over the other two will result in trying to sit on a three-legged stool with one leg longer than the others.

Activities are the common thread that links all continuous improvement tools... Total Quality Management, Process Reengineering, Time-Based Competition, Benchmarking and many more.

ACTIVITY BASED MANAGEMENT

Team Exercise:

Using the Activity Based information below, develop three ideas to improve productivity by 10%. Is there a difference in these ideas compared to those created using the traditional management accounting information on page 3?

RECEIVING DEPARTMENT	
Receive Material	$291,470
Move Material	302,940
Expedite Material	157,350
Manage Employees	138,140
Do Admin. Tasks	54,100
Total Cost	$944,000

Ideas

1. _____

2. _____

3. _____

Activity Based Management

The common theme throughout the principles of Excellence is a focus on activity information. A company must adopt an activity and process information system if they plan to achieve Excellence. Throughout the remainder of this book, we will refer to this activity and process information system as Activity Based Management (ABM).

Activity Based Management is the planning, improvement, and control of an organization's activities to meet customer and external requirements. Activity Based Management is essential to Excellence. Activities are what an organization does. Improvement is impossible without changing the activities performed by people and machines. Activity information provides the information to answer questions such as:

- How can I synchronize my activities with my supplier and customer?
- Does the person receiving the output want it? If not, it is non-value added.
- Is the activity primary to the mission or purpose of my department? Or, is it an administrative secondary activity?
- How can I change?
  - Activities performed   • Methods
  - Workload   • Resources
- How can I establish a culture that will motivate people to do their job well?
- How can I provide feedback on how well the activity is performed?

On the next two pages you will find a questionnaire designed to rate a company's ability to successfully implement ABM Continuous Improvement. Answer the questions and rate your company's readiness for Continuous Improvement. Discuss your answers with others in your department and senior management.

Tom Peters, in his very popular book In Search of Excellence defined eight attributes of an excellent organization. Combining Peters' eight attributes of Excellence with the basic principles of ABM produces a fresh and practical approach to continuous improvement:

1) *A bias for action...*
An activity based information system provides managers and employees a verb + noun language to continuously improve.

2) *Stay close to the customer...*
Employees should ask, "What are the customer requirements and expectations of my activities?"

3) *Autonomy and entrepreneurship...*
Employees should be empowered to make "improvements" to their departmental activities and "innovations" to business processes.

4) *Productivity through people...*
Continuously improve the cost per output of value added activities.

5) *Hands-on, value driven...*
Quantify value and non-value added activity costs.

6) *Stick to the knitting...*
Determine which activities and business processes represent the strategic core competencies of your organization.

7) *Simple form, lean staff...*
Limit the time and resources consumed by secondary administrative activities to no more than 10% of total costs.

8) *Simultaneous loose-tight control...*
The best performance measure is the one you do not need. In other words, make your business processes simple and mistake proof.

Rate Your Readiness For Continuous Improvement

Question 1: The fewer the levels of management, the more likely any Continuous Improvement initiative will succeed. Count how many layers of management exist between you and your company president. Score yourself:

    0 Points if there are more than 10 layers
    1 Point   if there are between 6-8 layers
    2 Points if there are between 4-6 layers
    3 Points if there are less than 4 layers

Question 2:   The sponsor of Continuous Improvement serves as a catalyst for change. The sponsor provides the necessary resources and time to implement Continuous Improvement. Who is your company's sponsor? Score yourself:

    0 Points If the sponsor is not a manager
    1 Point   If the sponsor is a manager
    2 Points If the sponsor is a mid-level executive
    3 Points If the sponsor is from a senior level (president, CEO, COO)

Question 3: An organization that has a strong sense of urgency for improvement backed by a corporate culture committed to Excellence will be highly motivated. Are you and your fellow employees motivated to change? Score yourself:

    0 Points If there is no corporate culture or little chance of survival
    1 Point   If there is some interest to improve
    2 Points If your management has stated "We will improve by 10% this year".
    3 Points If your company has committed to winning the Baldrige National Quality Award

Question 4:   A management team that asks questions on a regular basis about the improvement of activity and process cost, quality, and cycle time are more likely to succeed in implementing and sustaining Continuous Improvement. How often are you asked Activity questions? Score yourself:

    0 Points If your management never asks about Activities or Value
    1 Point   If your management asks once every few months
    2 Points If your management asks once a month
    3 Points If your management asks every day

Question 5: An organization that is provided Continuous Improvement education and training is more likely to succeed and sustain. Have you received any quality, cost improvement or process improvement training? Score yourself:

    0 Points If you have received no training
    1 Point   If you receive less than 4 hours training per year
    2 Points If you receive between 1-5 days training per year
    3 Points If you receive more than 5 days of Continuous Improvement training per year

Question 6: An organization that openly recognizes that they are not the best at every Activity or Business Process is more likely to accept Continuous Improvement change. Does your organization compare itself to others? Score yourself:

0 Points   If no outside comparisons are made
1 Point   If comparisons are limited to other sites or divisions of your company
2 Points   If you have an active benchmarking program
3 Points   If you have benchmarked and implemented best practice changes

Question 7: Does your organization encourage and implement new ideas? Score yourself:

0 Points   If management's attitude is "You can't have any good ideas.   You work for us."
1 Point   If your organization has an employee recommendation program
2 Points   If your organization has an employee recognition program for CIP ideas
3 Points   If new ideas that require no capital expenditure require few if any approvals

Question 8: Employees that have been bombarded with three letter acronym initiatives... such as TQM, JIT, BPR, DFM, and DFT... are naturally skeptical of change. How many projects have you been involved with? Score yourself:

0 Points   If you have seen initiatives come and go over the years
1 Point   If you have seen some success with one or more pilot projects, but then stopped
2 Points   If your organization has had some success sustaining one or more initiatives
3 Points   If your organization can easily point to significant results of initiatives

Question 9: Employees that participate in a Continuous Improvement Program will want to know what will be done with Non-Value Added resources. If they are not informed of a redeployment or elimination plan by senior management, they will likely roadblock CIP changes. Has your senior management addressed this issue? Score yourself:

0 Points   If you have not heard of a plan
1 Point   If you heard a plan, but don't trust or believe it
2 Points   If you heard a plan, but are cautiously optimistic
3 Points   If you have a plan that is practical and nonthreatening

Question 10: To effectively implement and sustain Continuous Improvement requires changing management's habits and attitudes. Is yours willing to change? Score yourself:

0 Points   If you think management will never stop classifying people as Direct or Indirect
1 Point   If your management has exhibited the willingness to change outdated performance measures
2 Points   If your management wants to empower employees with Activity Based Management information and the authority to act
3 Points   If your management visibly recognizes that every employee will do a good job if they enjoy their job

TOTAL

IF YOUR SCORE IS...

24-30   Continuous Improvement is likely to succeed. Strive for 30 points!!
16-23   Continuous Improvement is possible, but probably difficult. Focus on areas you scored lowest.
0-15   Continuous Improvement will be virtually impossible. Do a small pilot project to demonstrate a quick success.

Chapter Summary

Traditional Management leads companies to short-term quick-fix improvement. Traditional Management information systems focus on managing costs, not the work that consumes the cost. This hurts the organization's longevity by encouraging "easy fixes" to problems, and not enough emphasis on going back to the basics - do the right things and do them better than the competition.

There are five major principles to Excellence in Management:

1. Manage activities, not resources
2. Synchronize activities within business processes
3. Continually eliminate waste
4. Continually improve activity costs, quality, and response time
5. Empower employees to improve

Activity Based Management (ABM) is the planning, improvement, and control of an organization's activities to meet customer and external requirements. The activity and process information provided in an ABM system answers questions such as:

- How can I synchronize my activities with my supplier and customer?
- Does the person receiving the Output want it?
- Is the activity primary to the mission of the department?
- How can I change my activities performed, workload, methods and resources?
- How can I establish a culture to motivate the people to do their jobs well?
- How can I provide feedback on how well the activity is performed?

Read the next chapter to learn more about ABM.

 **Notes**

Activity Based Management

If your organization has already implemented ABM, use this chapter of the book to refresh your memory on ABM terminology and to compare your activity accounting reports to the format utilized in this book. If your company has not implemented ABM, use this chapter to prepare for activity analysis interviews and creating your department's activity accounting worksheet.

Before creating your Activity Based Management information system, you must first understand the ABM hierarchy of information. Focusing your improvement efforts solely at the function level is too general and can result in little or no improvement. Focusing attention at the Task level will result in an information system that is too tedious to maintain. As the name implies, the key to developing an Activity Based Management information system is to focus on Activities and the linkage of those Activities into Business Processes.

ABM is a process of simplification, not complication.

An ABM information system focuses on the seven to ten significant activities performed in each and every department and how those activities form ten to fifteen significant business processes.

ABM Heirarchy

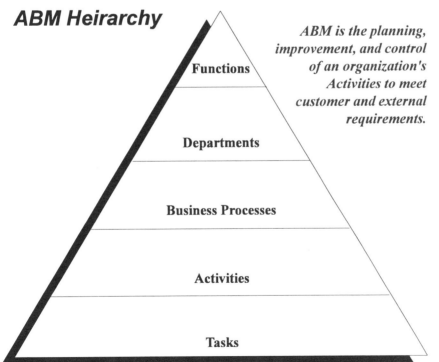

ABM is the planning, improvement, and control of an organization's Activities to meet customer and external requirements.

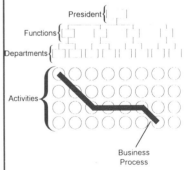

Function

A Function is a collection of people in one or more locations that share a common responsibility. The Sales Function has responsibility for selling the product. The Manufacturing Function has responsibility for making the product. Functions are typically listed at the top of an organizational chart. Functions often have a Vice President (i.e., VP of Sales, VP of Manufacturing, VP of Finance). Most organizations are organized "vertically" by function. As a result, employees view themselves as independent "silos" or cells working in competition, not together. A function is composed of several department or cost centers.

Department/Cost Center

A Department or Cost Center represents one portion of a function. A Department typically contains people and/or machines that share a common purpose or mission. Typically, a function has several departments, each with a specific responsibility or speciality.

Business Process

A Business Process is a collection of related activities operating under a set of procedures in order to accomplish a specific objective such as Process a Customer Order, Procure Raw Materials, Design a New Production, or Market Product.

Business Processes transcend standard departmental boundaries in an organization, forcing employees to realize that their customer is not the person who buys the final product... it is more often the next department. Employees begin to realize that performance of their activity, in terms of cost, time, and quality, has a domino effect on subsequent department's activities.

Activity

An Activity is a Verb + Noun description of what an organization does. A Department typically performs seven to ten significant activities. To aid in identifying the correct level of detail, remember the following:

A **"significant activity"** is one which consumes at least 5% but no more than 40% of the entire department's time.

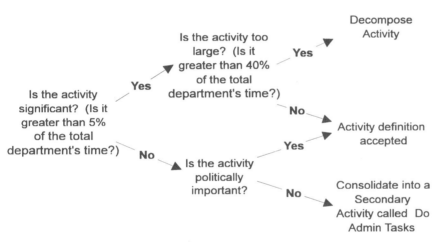

Example Activities

Receive Material
Issue Purchase Order
Move Materials
Attend Meetings
Take Order
Do Setup
Issue Report
Perform Test
Inspect Component
Issue Check

Task

Tasks are the steps necessary to perform an activity. An activity represents "What" an organization does. A task represents "How" an organization does it.

The identification of activity task information should come after you have established your ABM system. Task analysis of an activity is an excellent option to define improvements. Task analysis should be the responsibility of the people who do the Activity. Do not put tasks into your Activity Accounting system.

*Example Tasks of the
Activity "Receive Material"*

Count boxes
*Match Purchase Order to
Receipt*
Edit incorrect data
Sign Receiver Notice
Enter data into computer
File paperwork
*Mail copy to Accounts
Payable*

Activity Based Management

TIP:
More is not better. Do not think more activities make a better ABM system. Most companies can effectively describe themselves with 200-250 different activities.

An Activity...

Represents Time

Produces Outputs

Output
Consumes Resources

An Activity Based Management information system utilizes a simple, yet probably familiar, structure:

Activities are the foundation for an Activity Based Management information system.

An activity is a Verb and Noun description of what an organization does. An activity can be described in one of three ways:

(1) An Activity represents the way time is spent within a department or cost center. For example, the receiving department employees spend approximately 33% of their time "Receiving Material".

A **"Significant Activity"** is one which consumes at least 5% but no more than 40% of the entire department's time.

(2) An activity produces the output of the department. Output represents what internal or external customer(s) receive from your department. For example, an output of the Receiving Department is a Receiving Notice.

(3) An activity consumes the resources (cost) of a department to produce an output. Do not overlook activities performed by machines. Both machines and people do activities that consume resources.

Input

Each activity will have an Input. An Input is the factor(s) that "triggers" or "causes" the activity to occur. An activity can have one or more inputs. For example, the inputs for the activity "Receive Material" would be a Shipment of Raw Materials and a Bill of Lading.

Output

Once the input triggers the activity to occur, the activity begins to consume resources to produce an output. Each activity produces an output. The output represents the product of performing the activity. The output is what the department produces and what the internal/ external customer(s) receives from the department. The output for the activity "Receive Material" would be a "Receipt".

Output Measures

Associated with each activity output is a measure of activity workload, called an Output Measure. The output measure is a quantifiable measure for the output of an activity. The output measure for the activity "Receive Material" could be "Number of Receipts."

Do not use time based output measures:
Correct:
Number of bottles filled, or Number of equivalent 50 tablet bottles filled
Incorrect:
Number of minutes to fill bottle

Output Measure Guidelines
- To begin, put the words "Number of" in front of the Activity output to define the output measure.
- Assess whether the output measure is easy to collect. If not, define a surrogate measure.
- Determine whether the output is homogeneous. In other words, does the output take approximately the same amount of time or resources each time the Activity output is produced? If an output is not homogeneous, determine the factor that causes the variability and define an equivalent measure.
- Use only one output measure per Activity.

Each activity can be assigned Activity Characteristics to support your ABM analysis. The standard characteristics are Primary or Secondary and Value or Non-Value Added.

Activity Characteristics

Primary vs. Secondary

Primary activities contribute directly to the central mission of the department or organization. Primary activities for a Receiving department would be "Receive Material", "Move Material", and "Expedite Material". Typically, the output of a primary activity leaves the department or cost center.

Secondary activities support an organization's primary activities. They are administrative in nature and occur in almost every department. Typical secondary activities are: Manage Employees, Train Employees, Attend Meetings, and Do Administrative Tasks.

	Typical	
	Results	*Excellence*
Primary	*80%*	*90%*
Secondary	*20%*	*10%*

Primary vs. Secondary Analysis often exposes that an organization is spending too much time and costs on administrative activities. A typical Primary vs. Secondary Analysis reveals approximately 80% of an organization's resources are spent on primary activities and 20% on secondary. Your goal should be a 90%/10% ratio. A high secondary percentage is symptomatic of excessive bureaucracy and inappropriate spans of control. A low secondary percentage is symptomatic of no training, planning or effective communication. See page 63 for further discussion of Primary Analysis.

Value vs. Non-Value Added

A Value Added Activity is one required to meet customer or external requirements. Value added activities for a Receiving department would be "Receive Material," "Train Employees," and "Do Admin. Tasks." A Non-Value Added Activity is one not required to meet customer or external requirements. In other words, the activity equals waste. Non-Value added activities for a Receiving department would be "Move Material" and "Expedite Material."

	Typical	
	Results	*Excellence*
Value Added	*65%*	*100%*
Non-Value Added	*35%*	*0%*

Value vs. Non-Value Added Analysis often reveals an organization is spending approximately 65% of its resources on value added activities and 35% on non-value added. Your goal should be to drive the non-value added % to zero. See page 55 for added discussion on Value Analysis

Activity Dictionary

While each company, on the surface, is different from another, the typical Activities performed by each department in a company are very predictable. A great source for Activity information is an Activity Dictionary. Ask your C.I. Team leader, quality manager or accounting department if they have compiled an Activity dictionary for your organization.

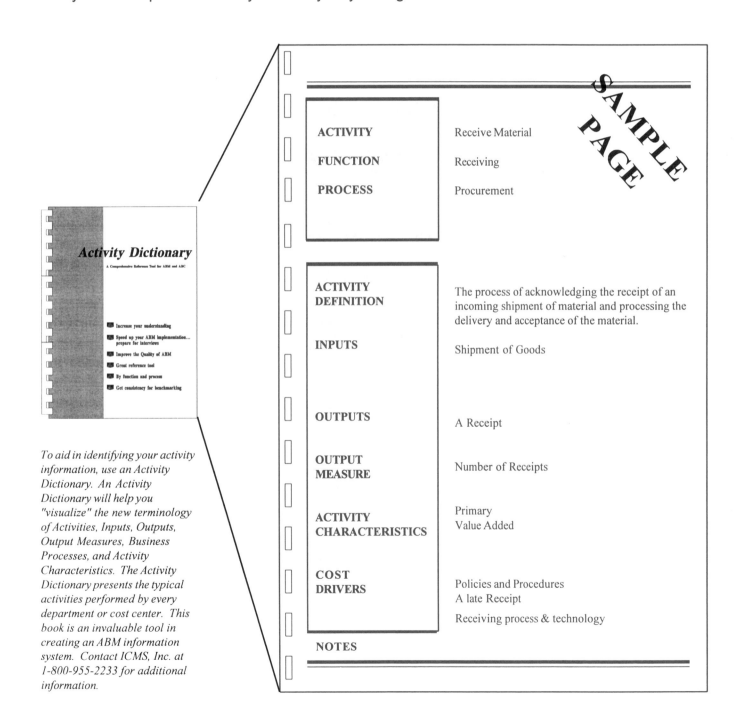

To aid in identifying your activity information, use an Activity Dictionary. An Activity Dictionary will help you "visualize" the new terminology of Activities, Inputs, Outputs, Output Measures, Business Processes, and Activity Characteristics. The Activity Dictionary presents the typical activities performed by every department or cost center. This book is an invaluable tool in creating an ABM information system. Contact ICMS, Inc. at 1-800-955-2233 for additional information.

The agenda for an Activity Analysis interview is as follows:

(A) *Review why ABM is being implemented*
15 minutes

(B) *Draft a 1 or 2 Sentence Departmental Mission Statement*
5 minutes

(C) *Define Department Outputs*
30 minutes

(D) *Define Department Activities, Inputs, Output Measures and Time Percentages*
45 minutes

(E) *Identify Continuous Improvement suggestions*
15 minutes

(F) *Wrap-up*
5 minutes

Creating an ABM Information System

Step 1 -Activity Analysis

The first step in creating your ABM information system is defining the activities for each department or cost center. The process of identifying what an organization does is called Activity Analysis. Activity Analysis decomposes an organization into its significant activities.

The goal of Activity Analysis is to define for each department or cost center the following:

- 7-10 Significant Activities
- Estimated Time Percentage spent on each Activity
- Activity Input(s), Outputs and Output Measures
- Classify Activities as Primary or Secondary and Value or Non-Value Added
- Link Activities to a Business Process

Benefits of Activity Analysis:

- Provides managers and employees with a clear view of the department's workload profile
- Clarifies customer & supplier relationships including cross-departmental processes
- Provides a basis for continuous improvement
- Provides a basis for improved planning and budgeting

There are several methods for collecting Activity Analysis information, but the most commonly used is a departmental interview (see sidebar for the agenda). An Activity Analysis interview typically lasts two hours and involves a cross section of department employees. A sample list of Activity Analysis interview questions can be found on the following page.

Activity Analysis Interview Questions

1. Describe in one or two sentences the purpose or mission of your department.

2. What are the outputs of the department and who is the customer of each output?

3. What are the time consuming, costly and labor intensive activities the department performs to produce these outputs? (Activities that consume at least 5% of the department's time or resources.)

4. Are there any non-repetitive activities that take place during the year (i.e., Do Budget)? Are there any Secondary Administrative Activities such as Manage Employees, Train Employees, or Do Administrative Tasks?

5. Is there significant waiting or downtime associated with the department (i.e., wait for repairs)?

6. What is the % of time spent on each Activity?

7. What is the input for each of these activities? Are the input(s) caused by outputs from another department?

8. Identify an output measure for each Activity. Note: You will be requested to collect the output measure quantity.

9. Are the Activities primary or secondary?

10. Are the Activities Value or Non-Value Added? (Hint: Put "Re" in front of each Activity. Do you ever have to "Re-do" a Value Added Activity?)

Activity Analysis Interview

■ Who leads the interviews and asks the ten questions?

The interview should be performed by two people. One is typically the project leader creating the ABM information system. The other person helps write down the information. This person can be a member of the ABM information system project team or one of the members of the department being interviewed.

■ Who should be interviewed?

In a department of less than ten people, involve everyone in the interview. In a large department, interview one person from each job classification.

■ Why explain ABM?

Employees want and need to know if ABM is a tool for them to use or a "club" that will be used on them. The person leading the interview should explain why the company has decided to implement an ABM information system. Magazine articles and/or books on ABM should be made available to those employees wishing additional information on ABM.

■ What is a Department Mission Statement?

It is a brief description created by the department's employees defining in one or two sentences the purpose of their department.

Example:

Accounts Payable: Process payments to our suppliers and employees.
Sales: Solicit orders from customers.

■ What is a good way to define department outputs?

Outputs are the "products" of the department.

Draw a box that represents the department. Ask the employees in the interview to define what outputs leave the department.

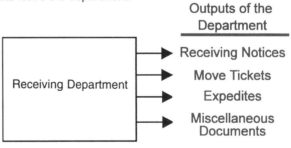

How do I define activities?

If there is an output, there is typically an activity. Therefore, for each output, describe using a verb and noun, the activity that produces the output (i.e., "Receive Material" is the activity that produces the output "Receiving Notices.")

Do all activities have an output?

No. Most do, but some secondary (administrative) activities do not. Don't overlook non-repetitive and secondary activities in the interview.

How do I gather the activity time percentage?

Don't do time and motion studies!! Simply ask each person or one person from each job classification (in a department of more than ten people) to estimate how much of their time is spent on each activity in the department. Account for 100%!!

What is an "inactivity?"

Don't overlook time spent on waiting (i.e., Wait for Order, Wait for Maintenance, Wait for Approval, etc.). If waiting consumes more than 5% of a department's time, include the "wait" inactivity on your activity analysis worksheet.

What is an input?

An input is what triggers or causes the activity. Inputs can be (1) physical, like a document or delivery; (2) electronic, like a phone call or E-mail; or (3) a policy. The input most often comes from outside your department. Inputs are used for Root Cause Analysis.

How do you define the output measure of each activity?

For primary activities, the output measure can be defined by simply putting the words "Number of" in front of the activity output. For example, if the output is "A Receipt," the output measure is "Number of Receipts."

For secondary activities, the simplest output measure is always "Number of Employees." Employees are not the output of the activity "Do Admin. Tasks," but by using Number Of Employees for every secondary activity in every department, you will get a relevant cost per output to compare between departments.

Make sure the output measure is practical to collect and homogenous.

Who should classify the activities as primary or secondary?

The employees in each department should classify their own activities. Determine primary or secondary by comparing each activity to the departmental mission statement. If the output of an Activity leaves the department, the Activity is typically Primary.

Who should classify the activities as value or non-value?

The employees in each department should classify their own activities.

Activity Based Management

As you ask the 10 questions on page 21, the objective of an Activity Analysis interview is to complete the sample form below for each department or cost center.

Activity Analysis Worksheet						
Department Receiving			**Person Interviewed** All Employees			
Purpose Receive and Deliver Raw Materials			**Interviewers** Chris and Dick			
Input	**Activity Description**	**Output**	**Output Measure**	**Time %**	**Primary/ Secondary**	**Value/ Non-Value**
Shipment of Goods	Receive Material	A Receipt	Number of Receipts	33%	P	V
Move Ticket	Move Material	A Move Ticket	Number of Moves	26%	P	NV
A Request	Expedite Material	An Expedite	Number of Expedites	15%	P	NV
Policy	Manage Employees	A Supervised Employee	Number of Employees	20%	S	V
A Request	Do Admin. Tasks	Miscellaneous Document	Number of Employees	6%	S	V

Blank forms of the above worksheet are provided at the end of the chapter.

Step 2 - Activity Accounting

The process of tracing departmental resources or costs to an activity is called Activity Accounting. Activity Accounting is based on the simple concept that activities consume costs.

The second step in creating your ABM information system is to trace to each activity the departmental resources required to perform the activity. For example, to perform the activity "Receive Material", the following resources are required:

- ◆ Supplies
- ◆ Equipment
- ◆ People
- ◆ Floorspace
- ◆ Telephones

As with the Activity Analysis process, a departmental interview is the most commonly used method for gathering the Activity Accounting information. The interview should involve the individual responsible for preparing the departmental budget, typically the manager or supervisor. The interview should last approximately one hour. A typical Activity Accounting interview and worksheet follows.

❶

SUPPLIES:
Approximately 40% of our supplies budget is spent on receiving forms. We spend approximately 17% for move tickets, 24% for expedite forms, 7% for office supplies, and 12% for miscellaneous forms.

❷

DEPRECIATION:
Reviewing the asset reports in accounting, $110,000 is for the forklifts to move material, $35,000 is for computers to receive, $35,000 is for computers to expedite, $3,000 is for the manager's office equipment, and $3,000 is for miscellaneous office equipment.

Activity Accounting Worksheet		Activities				
		Receive Material	Move Material	Expedite Material	Manage Employees	Do Admin Tasks
Cost	Total	Primary / Value Secondary / Non-Value	Primary / Value Secondary / Non-Value	Primary / Value Secondary / Non-Value	Primary / Value Secondary / Non-Value	Primary / Value Secondary / Non-Value
❶ Supplies	$88,000	$ 35,200	$ 15,000	$ 21,000	$ 6,240	$ 10,560
❷ Depreciation	$186,000	35,000	110,000	35,000	3,000	3,000
❸ Salaries	$545,000	179,850	141,700	81,750	109,000	32,700
❹ Space	$51,000	17,000	17,000	8,500	5,100	3,400
❺ All Other	$74,000	24,420	19,240	11,100	14,800	4,440
Total Cost	$944,000	$ 291,470	$ 302,940	$ 157,350	$ 138,140	$ 54,100
Output Measure Quantity		2,500	11,000	1,250	10	10
Output Measure		# of Receipts	# of Moves	# of Expedites	# of Employees	# of Employees
❻ Cost per Output		$ 117	$ 28	$ 126	$ 13,814	$ 5,410

❸

SALARIES:
Assign these costs using the Activity time percentages defined during Activity Analysis:

Receive Material	33%
Move Material	26%
Expedite Material	15%
Manage Employees	20%
Do Admin. Tasks	6%
	100%

❹

SPACE:
Assign this cost on square footage. The total sq. ft. of the department is 1,000 sq. ft. We use 330 sq. ft. for the receiving dock, 330 sq. ft. for the staging area, and 340 sq. ft. for the office. Assume 170 sq. ft. for the expeditor's office, and 100 sq. ft. for the manager's office, and approximately 70 sq. ft. for the clerical space.

❺

ALL OTHER:
The remainder of the budget, such as telephone and postage, is not really traceable to any specific activity. Allocate "All Other" using the time percentages.

Activity Based Management

Activity Accounting Tips

■ *Use actual costs. It is easier to collect output measure volumes for past time periods than to estimate quantities for a future period.*

■ *Analyze an entire year. Eliminate the impact of seasonal factors.*

■ *Group cost and expense accounts in each department that have a common cost tracing behavior pattern. The goal is to have fewer than 12 cost groupings per department. For example, combine Salary, Payroll Taxes, Holiday Pay, Vacation Pay, and Sick Pay into one account called Salary Expenses. By doing so, you reduce the number of cost tracing calculations from five to one.*

■ *Have each department collect their own output measure volumes.*

The final step of Activity Accounting is to calculate each Activity Cost per Output. This is done by dividing the Total Activity Cost by the Total Output Measure Quantity.

For example, the cost per output of the activity Receive Material (page 25) is $117. For the example, we have rounded to the nearest dollar.

❻
$$\frac{Total\ Cost\ of\ Activity}{Total\ Output\ Quantity\ of\ Activity} = \frac{Cost\ Per\ Output\ of}{the\ Activity}$$

$$\frac{\$291,470}{2,500\ Receipts} = \$117\ per\ Receipt$$

The Activity Based Management information on page 25 is necessary to support the Five Step Continuous Improvement Process.
You should have available to you before proceeding with continuous improvement:

■ Activities defined for each department
■ Gross cost of each activity
■ Quantity of output for each activity
■ Cost per output

An Activity Based Management information system supports continuous improvement tools such as...

...Value Analysis
...Benchmarking
...Process Mapping & Redesign
...Root Cause Analysis
...Activity Based Budgeting
...Total Quality Management
...Performance Measurements

Note: The ABM information you have created can also be used for ABC product costing. Using ABM information for more accurate allocation of cost to products has little to do with continuous improvement, and therefore, is not covered in this text.

What are your Department's Activities?

Fill out your own department's Activity Analysis and Activity Accounting worksheets presented below and on the following page.

Activity Analysis Worksheet						
Department_____ Purpose_____			Person Interviewed_____ Interviewer(s) _____			
Input	**Activity Description**	**Output**	**Output Measure**	**Time %**	**Primary/ Secondary**	**Value/ Non-Value**
				100%		

Activity Based Management

Activity Accounting Worksheet

Activities

Cost	Total	Primary / Value Secondary / Non-Value	Primary / Value Secondary / Non-Value	Primary / Value Secondary / Non-Value	Primary / Value Secondary / Non-Value	Primary / Value Secondary / Non-Value	Primary / Value Secondary / Non-Value	Primary / Value Secondary / Non-Value
	$	$	$	$	$	$	$	$
Total Cost	$	$	$	$	$	$	$	$
Output Measure Quantity								
Output Measure								
Cost per Output		$	$	$	$	$	$	$

Discuss your department's ABM information with your fellow Continuous Improvement Team (C.I. Team) members. Your team can be comprised of all or a cross section of your department.

What observations do you have about your department's Activities and Activity Costs?

1) _____

_____

_____

2) _____

_____

_____

3) _____

_____

_____

4) _____

_____

_____

5) _____

_____

_____

Chapter Summary

An Activity Based Information System begins with the basics:

Activity:
- ◆ Described as a verb + noun
- ◆ How we spend time
- ◆ Consumes cost
- ◆ Typically 7-10 per department

Input:
- ◆ Triggers an activity to occur
- ◆ May be more than one input per activity
- ◆ Normally provided by another department or outside supplier

Output:
- ◆ The product of an activity
- ◆ Can be physical or electronic data
- ◆ May be more than one output per activity

Output Measure:
- ◆ Number of times an activity is performed
- ◆ Only one output measure per activity
- ◆ Not a measure of time

Activity Characteristics are ways to classify your activities. There are four basic activity characteristics: Primary, Secondary, Value Added and Non-Value Added. **Primary activities** contribute directly to the central mission of the department or organization. **Secondary activities** support the primary activities and are typically administrative in nature. **Value Added activities** are required to meet customer or external requirements. **Non-Value Added activities** are not required to meet customer or external requirements.

A **Business Process** is a sequence or network of dependent activities performed to achieve a specific objective.

To create an ABM Information System, you must perform Activity Analysis and Activity Accounting.

 **Notes**

Continuous Improvement Process

Jack's Visit to the Idea Doctor

Jack's mind felt like a head of wilted lettuce. He'd just returned from a meeting with his boss and found out that he wouldn't be getting the promotion he'd been hoping for. As he thought about his situation, Jack realized that he hadn't been performing very well lately. He had missed deadlines on several crucial projects. And his once perceptive mind was producing trite solutions to important problems.

He tried to put some pizzazz back into his thinking, but nothing worked. Finally, he went to an idea doctor for help. "I just don't seem to have it anymore, Jack explained. The doctor explained he was going to ask a few questions so that he could determine the correct diagnosis to Jack's problem.

"First, have you stuck your neck out and taken any risks lately?"

"Not that I can remember," Jack answered.

"Have you been asking 'What If' to stretch your imagination?"

"I've been too busy."

"Have you kept an open mind when evaluating new ideas?"

"I know what works and what doesn't."

The questioning went on like this for a while. Finally Jack asked, "What is the diagnosis?"

"No doubt about it, you are stuck in a rut." The doctor proclaimed, "You've got your ends reversed."

"What?" Jack responded.

"You see, the human body has two ends on it - one to create ideas and one to sit on. As long as you actively pursue new ideas, your creative end stays in good shape. But if you sit around doing the same old things, your brain descends into your rear. As a result, your ends get reversed."

Continuous Improvement Process

When asked what single event was most helpful in developing the theory of relativity, Albert Einstein is reported to have answered, "Figuring out how to think about the problem."

This story is from the book, "A Kick In the Seat of the Pants," by Roger von Oech. This story illustrates two issues confronting most organizations and their employees: (1) You cannot improve what you take for granted, and (2) You cannot improve what you don't understand.

If assembling a giant jigsaw puzzle were approached in the manner most managers approach the Continuous Improvement Process (CIP), you would see pieces flying everywhere with many groups of two or three pieces fitted together, but nothing that resembled a complete picture. A disciplined Five Step Continuous Improvement approach that utilizes the common verb + noun language of an Activity Based Management information system brings out the best of our *past* knowledge, the best of our *current* creative talents and analytical skills to achieve a *future* goal of Excellence.

Five Steps to Continuous Improvement

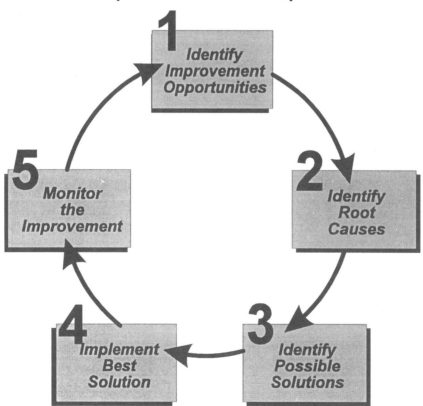

Employees that are provided a practical tool like ABM, coupled with a continuous improvement target can produce startling results. Employees working together on Continuous Improvement Teams (C.I. Teams) focused on Activity information, can meet the challenges required to achieve Excellence.

The following pages provide an overview to the Five Steps to Continuous Improvement. Each step will be fully explained in following chapters and the Appendices.

Step 1 - Identify Improvement Opportunities

There are two parts to approaching any opportunity or solving a problem. First, admit you have a need to improve and second, define logical steps to address the need.

The first step in your Continuous Improvement Process will be to identify opportunities for improvement. The remaining steps focus on how you want to do it. Before investing valuable time and resources, the Continuous Improvement (C.I.) Team must have a clear direction for their Continuous Improvement efforts. Do we want to reduce our Non-Value Added cost? Do we want to improve our Primary/Secondary ratio? Do we want to improve the quality of a Value Added Activity?

By clearly defining opportunities for improvement, the C.I. Team will steer clear of the typical **Continuous Improvement Pitfalls**, such as:

- Solving the wrong problem
- Underestimating employee resistance to change
- Solving the symptom and not the Root Cause
- Setting an improvement goal too low
- Agreeing on a solution before there is an agreement on the need for improvement.

Steps To Continuous Improvement
1. Identify Improvement Opportunities
2. Identify Root Cause
3. Identify Possible Solutions
4. Implement Best Solution
5. Monitor the Improvement

Avoid Continuous Improvement Pitfalls

Continuous Improvement Process

"What we take for granted we give up the possibility of changing or improving."

Richard Wurman
"Information Anxiety"

So, where should we look for these improvement opportunities to come from??? Your Activity Based Management information system, of course. The decision tree below illustrates the available options for identifying your Continuous Improvement opportunities.

Decision Trees:
One barrier to finding something is not knowing what you want. By defining alternative routes, Decision Trees ensure your decision is correct by making sure you ask the appropriate questions.

The decision tree for identifying improvement opportunities takes two distinctive paths: Activity vs. Process improvement. Activity improvement is most commonly performed by a departmental or functional employee C.I. Team. Process improvement, on the other hand, involves numerous functional areas and should be approached using a multifunctional C.I. Team. Deciding which direction to take will depend on your organization's goals or objectives.

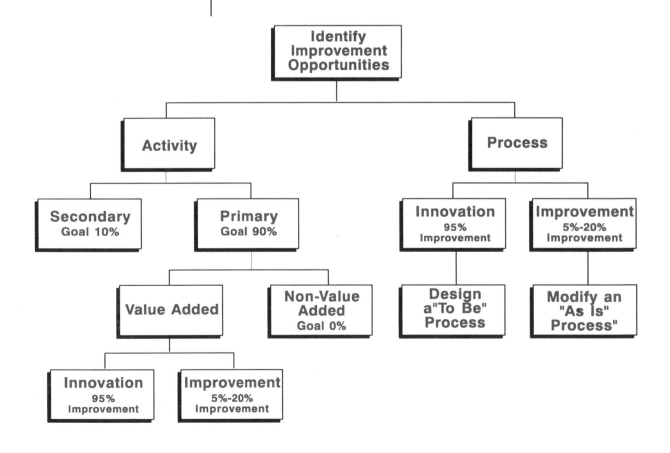

Activity Improvement

There are four basic avenues for improving an activity. The option that is suitable for you will depend upon your specific goals and objectives.

Option 1 - Improving your Primary/Secondary Ratio
A typical Primary vs. Secondary Analysis reveals an organization is spending too much time and money on administrative activities. Your goal should be to maintain a ratio of 90% of your resources spent on Primary Activities and 10% spent on Secondaries. If your department or organization is spending in excess of the desired 90/10 ratio, **Secondary Improvement** could be an area to focus your efforts.

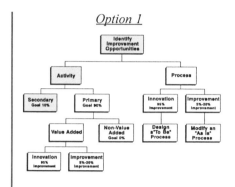

Option 1

Option 2 - Elimination of a Non-Value Added Activity
A typical Value Analysis reveals an organization is spending approximately 65% of its resources on activities, which add value to its products and processes. Therefore, 35% is spent on activities that add no value (Non-Value Added) to the organization. Your goal should be to drive your Non-Value Added % to zero. The goal is not expected to be achievable, but it provides a target so that an organization is never satisfied unless it is reducing its **Non-Value Added** cost by substantial amounts year after year.

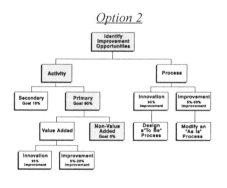

Option 2

Option 3 - Innovating a Value Added Activity
Innovating an activity involves performing the activity in a radically new way. For example, installing a bar coding system to enhance the activity "Receive Material". The typical goal in **Activity Innovation** is a 95% improvement in the activity's cost, time or quality.

Note: Just because your Primary vs. Secondary ratio is within the reasonable limits and your Value vs. Non-Value Analysis reveals a relatively low Non-Value Added cost does not mean your opportunities for improvement are non-existent.

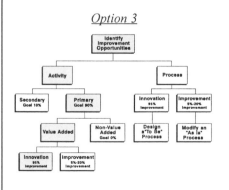

Option 3

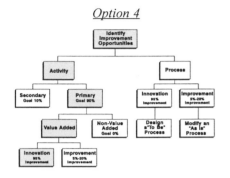

Option 4

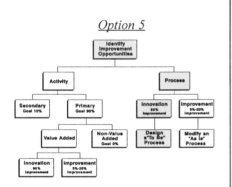

Option 5

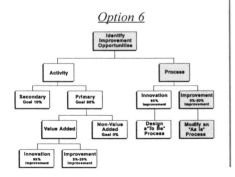

Option 6

Option 4 - Incrementally Improving a Value Added Activity

Incremental improvement of an activity typically involves performing the activity slightly different. The best way to incrementally improve an activity is to perform a "task analysis". A task analysis often exposes the non-value cost steps hidden within a value added activity. The typical goal of **Activity Improvement** is a 5% - 20% improvement.

Process Improvement

There are two basic avenues available for improving a Process.

    Option 5   Innovating a Process
    Option 6   Incrementally Improving a Process

Process Improvement involves questioning the existing business processes existing within your organization today. Since business processes transcend functional or department boundaries, the C.I. Team should be multifunctional. Business process improvements can take two forms: Process Improvement or Process Innovation.

Option 5 -Innovating a Process

Process Innovation is performing the existing Business Process in some radically new way. The goal of Process Innovation is a 95% productivity improvement. Process Innovations typically lead to changes in an organization's structure and culture.

Option 6 - Incrementally Improving a Process

Process Improvement involves performing the same business processes with only slightly increased efficiency or effectiveness. This option typically leads to a 5%-20% improvement in the process cost, time or quality. Incrementally improving a process might include: eliminating duplicate activities, simplifying activities, streamlining the process, and synchronizing activities within the process.

Management is responsible for setting the improvement percentage target and timeframe for completion. The C.I. Team will identify which of the six options best meets the target by using analysis tools such as:

-     Value Analysis
-     Primary Analysis
-     Business Process Analysis
-     Benchmarking

Step 2 - Identity Root Causes

Root Causes impact the cost, quality and time of an activity or process. The root cause of an activity or process is often generated by the output of activities performed by individuals who are not aware of the impact of their work. For example, the problem of poor quality might be the result of a purchasing department whose goal or performance measure is to keep the purchase price of raw materials at a minimum. Because of this goal, the purchasing department might sacrifice the quality of raw materials for a lower price. In the long run, the overall company suffers because of additional activities performed to correct the poor quality (i.e. Inspect Raw Materials, Process Scrap, Return Raw Materials, etc.). Other significant activity root causes typically uncovered in Step 2 are:

Continuous Improvement requires a commitment to Excellence...
    (1) Where are we?
    (2) Where can we be?
    (3) Are we getting there?

    (1) large number of raw material part numbers;
    (2) large number of products;
    (3) large number of customers.

The most useful and effective continuous improvement tools for this step are:

- Cause and Effect Diagramming
- Pareto Analysis
- 5 Whys Technique

Step 3 - Identify Possible Solutions

Often the search for the solution to a problem results in something totally unexpected. For example, Alexander Graham Bell was trying to invent a hearing aid when he invented the telephone, and Christopher Columbus was searching for India when he discovered a new world. Thus, it is important when solutions to the improvement issue are being generated that the C.I. Team be allowed to stray. Later, the group can evaluate the ideas for reasonableness.

Continuous Improvement Process

To avoid leaping to one solution, the C.I. Team should use continuous improvement tools such as:

- Brainstorming
- Storyboarding

Step 4 - Implement Best Solutions

The C.I. Team should select the solution which has the greatest impact on the problem. A Solution Rating Matrix is the most commonly used continuous improvement tool for selecting a solution to implement.

Once the C.I. Team has selected which solutions to implement, they should develop a plan consisting of the resources and time requirements necessary for implementation.

Step 5 - Monitor the Improvement

The C.I. Team should ask themselves, "How well did the solution work?" and "What else can be done?" The C.I. Team should establish an ongoing evaluation process using Continuous Improvement tools such as:

- ABM Performance Measures
- Activity Based Budgeting

If the solution was not successful, try an alternative. Remember, Continuous Improvement is an unending process.

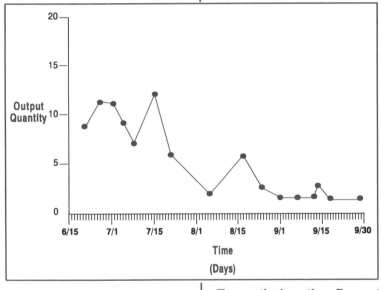

To optimize the five steps, you will need a team of fellow employees and a leader. Read pages 41-45 to organize your C.I. Team.

Continuous Improvement Teams (C.I. Teams)

The main purpose of this handbook is to get teams of employees focused on Activities and working towards Continuous Improvement. When teams of employees are given a common sense information based on activities, along with the Continuous Improvement tools discussed on pages 38-40, great things can happen. If you already participate on a team, review pages 41-45 for improvement ideas. If you do not currently participate on a team, start one!.

We recommend three types of teams to support your organization's Continuous Improvement process:

    1)   Departmental C.I. Teams;
    2)   Process C.I. Teams; and
    3)   A C.I. Committee.

The C.I. Team, whether it represents a department or process, performs the bulk of the work, carries out assignments and makes continuous improvement suggestions. An organization can have numerous C.I. Teams working at one time. A C.I. Team should consist of 4-7 employees from one functional area. If the Activity or Process targeted for improvement involves more that one functional area, it is recommended that the C.I. Team consist of employees from each of the areas effected. Members of the C.I. Team are responsible for:

- Attending all C.I. Team meetings
- Interview Employees and Customers
- Gather Data
- Make Improvement Suggestions.
- Implement Solutions and Measure Results
- Carry Out Assignments Given By the C.I. Team Leader

Each C.I. Team should have a C.I. Leader, responsible for managing the continuous improvement efforts of the C.I. team. This individual is responsible for facilitating meetings, handling or assigning administrative details, orchestrating all team activities, and overseeing the preparation of the final report and presentation. The C.I. Leader can be the department manager, an employee volunteer or a full-time C.I. facilitator that works with all teams.

We also recommend a senior management **C.I. Committee** to oversee the continuous improvement efforts of all C.I. Teams. The C.I. Committee consists of four to six members with diverse skills and resources, who have a stake in the continuous improvement process, and have the necessary authority to approve or make the changes recommended by the C.I. Teams.

The C.I. Committee's duties include:

- Identify the continuous improvement targets and timeframes
- Provide needed resources and budget
- Make policy decisions
- Recruit an ABM trainer or coach

The C.I. Committee should meet regularly with the C.I. Team. When necessary, the C.I. Committee may "run interface" for the C.I. Team, presenting the team's interests to the rest of the company. Lastly, the C.I. Committee ensures changes recommended by the C.I. Team are implemented and synchronized between improvement teams.

ABM Coach

Many organizations find that C.I. Teams function more effectively if they are assisted by people with extra training and hands-on experience in the concepts and principles of Activity Based Management. This person is referred to as the ABM Advisor or ABM Coach. Their primary responsibility is to instruct the C.I. Team and its leader on the basic principles of Activity Based Management, answer questions, push the team to act, and compare results to other companies.

The ABM Coach's purpose is to aid the C.I. Team members in discovering for themselves what the answers are, not to dictate answers. The ABM Coach will attend team meetings, but is neither a leader nor a team member. They are facilitators for the team and should, therefore, maintain a "neutral" position. The ABM Coach can initially be an outside consultant, but long term the coach should be one or more employees trained in ABM and Continuous Improvement techniques.

C.I. Team Meetings

There should be two types of meetings held on a regular basis to support the unending continuous improvement process:

    1)   Weekly C.I. Team Meetings
    2)   C.I. Work Sessions

Weekly C.I. Team Meetings - The C.I. Team will need to meet on a weekly basis. This meeting serves as the formal setting for the team's C.I. Team activities. It will be during these sessions that the C.I. Team will handle the administrative issues of the project. The initial C.I. Team meeting should last 2 - 3 hours. Once Continuous Improvement becomes a part of the corporate culture, the meeting will typically last from 1 to 2 hours.

During the first meeting, the ABM Coach, C.I. Team leader, a representative from the C.I. committee, and department employees should review and discuss the following items:

- **The written goals set forth from the C.I. Committee.**
  What are the targets for continuous improvement? Select who will participate on the team. If practical, begin with all department employees on the team. Do you anticipate any controversial issues? List your questions and arrange a meeting with the management team to get the answers.

- **Clarify roles**
  What responsibilities will each of you have? How will you communicate and coordinate with each other? Select a date for the weekly meetings.

- **Identify pertinent existing data**
  Review previous work in this area. To understand the present process, you must understand the history. Find out how the process came to be designed the way it is. Determine if anyone is currently collecting data on the activities or process you intend to study. Does Activity Accounting data exist? If not, create it.

Continuous Improvement Process

Meeting minutes should contain several types of information:

- *Date and Time of Meeting*
- *Names of Attendees*
- *Topics discussed*
- *Points discussed regarding each topic*
- *Action taken or decisions made regarding each topic*
- *Next steps for each topic*
- *Topics for future agendas*

■ **Set ground rules**

Have team members discuss ground rules for what the group will expect in terms of general courtesy (such as not interrupting conversations) and team member's responsibility for their behavior (such as promptness, smoking, carrying out assignments).

■ **Agendas, Minutes, and Records**

The C.I. Team leader is responsible for keeping the records of team meetings: agendas, minutes, reports, and so forth. However, teams often rotate the responsibility for taking minutes, writing reports, and sometimes setting agendas. Decide how these issues will be handled. Also consider how team members can amend these records and how they can get access to them.

C.I. Work Sessions - The second type of meeting will involve the C.I. Team and selected employees from the areas being impacted by the Activity or Process in review. During these sessions, the C.I. team will use the various Continuous Improvement tools (Brainstorming, Storyboarding, Cause-and-Effect Diagramming, etc.) to target a specific Activity or Process for Continuous improvement.

Each C.I. work session should have an agenda. It should be sent to participants in advance, if possible. If an agenda has not been developed before a meeting, spend the first five or ten minutes writing one on a flipchart. There are proposed agendas at the beginning of each section of the Five Steps in this book. Please refer to these when preparing the agenda for your C.I. work session.

In each C.I. work session you may want to involve the ABM coach or appoint a facilitator to be the C.I. Team Leader. The facilitator's chief responsibilities are:

- Keep the discussion focused on the topic;
- Explaining the continuous improvement tool to be used;
- Intervene if the discussion fragments into multiple conversations or issues;
- Prevent anyone from dominating the conversation or being overlooked;
- Bring discussions to a close.

A key part of the Continuous Improvement Process is to follow up with employees on the status of their suggestions or ideas. After the meeting, send each participant a summary of the meeting and follow that with any additional information or feedback that arises.

C.I. Meeting Rules of Etiquette

- ***Attendance:*** *Teams should place a high priority on meetings, regarding them as almost sacred.*
- ***Promptness:*** *Meetings should start and end on time, which makes it easier on everyone's schedules and avoids wasting time.*
- ***Meeting place and time:*** *Specify a regular meeting time and place, and establish a procedure for notifying members of meetings.*
- ***Participation:*** *Each member's viewpoint is valuable and they can make a unique contribution to the project. Emphasize the importance of both speaking freely and listening attentively. Structure discussions so that everyone contributes.*
- ***Basic conversational courtesies:*** *Listen attentively and respectfully to others. Don't interrupt.*
- ***Smoking and breaks:*** *Decide whether and under what circumstances smoking will be allowed, when to take breaks, and how long the breaks will be.*
- ***Interruptions:*** *Decide when interruptions (phone calls, for example) will and won't be tolerated.*

Chapter Summary

Five Steps to Continuous Improvement

1. Define the Continuous Improvement Opportunity... state the opportunity concisely and clearly to avoid pitfalls such as solving the wrong problem. Review and evaluate activities and business processes for improvement.

2. Identify the root cause of the activity or process... sometimes the root cause that causes the activity or process is not obvious. Use systematic problem solving techniques to pinpoint causes.

3. Identify possible solutions... generate a broad list of possible solutions. The best solution may be totally unexpected, and other times may be obvious and easy to overlook.

4. Develop a plan to implement the best solution... once the team has developed a list of possible solutions, decide which solution has the highest probability of success.

   Implement the action plan... be sure to follow the plan.

5. Measure the improvement... develop performance measures to continually evaluate the progress, verifying that the improvement has been implemented and is effective. If not successful, implement an alternative.

Problem solving and Continuous Improvement requires creativity, patience, discipline, continuous improvement, honesty, facts, and continuous learning to be successful.

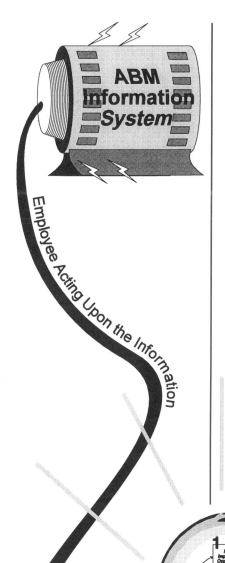

 **Notes**

Step 1: Identify Improvement Opportunities

Meeting Notes

Attendees:
C.I. Team members

Objective:
Define opportunities
for improvement
- Focus on Activity
- Focus on Process

Meeting Time:
2 hours

Supplies:
- Completed Activity
  Analysis worksheets
- Completed Activity
  Accounting
  worksheets

Meeting Agenda

■ Agree to meeting agenda and meeting length

■ Review and discuss the completed Activity Analysis & Activity Accounting information for the department or process.

■ Pre-read and then review Continuous Improvement Process chapter

■ Pre-read and then review the following chapters:
- Value Analysis
- Primary Analysis
- Business Process Analysis
- Benchmarking

■ Select an activity or process for Continuous Improvement

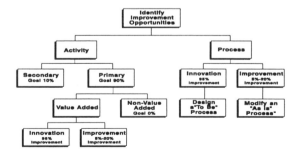

■ Define "To Do's" and people assignments for Step 2 – Identify Root Causes.

■ Define next meeting date and time.

■ Wrap-up.

Identify Improvement Opportunities

Only 20% of the companies that create an Activity Based Management information system consider the project a success. Why is the percentage so low? Why can only 20% specifically point to quantifiable benefits achieved as a result of implementing ABM? There is never one single root cause for a result like this. Most employees view ABM information, such as the Activity Accounting reports discussed in the previous chapter, as common sense, practical, and understandable. What then is preventing the use of the ABM information to achieve actual benefits? To successfully convert ABM findings into actual results requires three key ingredients:

- *Targets*
- *Timeframe*
- *Training*

Target

First, employees need a continuous improvement target. They need a goal. A target, whether the C.I. Team agrees with it or not, brings focus and action. For example, employees of General Electric are expected to achieve a 10% productivity improvement target each and every year.

What is an appropriate ABM continuous improvement target? Should your goal be a 5%, 10% or 20% improvement in your department's activities? Initially, the target for your organization should be defined by your senior management team. Beyond the first year, everyone in the organization should actively participate in the goal setting process. This chapter of the book covers four tools for both management and employees to utilize when defining continuous improvement targets: Value Analysis, Primary Analysis, Process Analysis and Benchmarking.

We begin the Continuous Improvement Process with:

- *Targets*

- *Timeframe*

- *Training*

Management should consider three factors when defining the improvement target.

1) What is the current financial condition of the entire organization? Are we currently making a profit? Are we achieving a reasonable return on our investment? If the organization is losing money, the target will potentially be higher the first year than in future years;

2) How do we compare to our competition? Are we the low cost provider of products and services in our industry? How does our quality compare to the competition? What is the customer's perception? Do our processes take more time than the average in our marketplace? Answers to these questions will focus targets on cost, time or quality and define the margin of improvement required to match or exceed the competition and customer expectations;

3) What is the organization's strategy? What are our strengths and weaknesses as an organization? What activities and processes do we perform better or worse than the competition? Which activities and processes could we exploit to our advantage in the marketplace? Which activities or processes should we reduce and redeploy for some other use?

Timeframe

To successfully achieve a target requires a timeframe or sense of urgency. If your organization needs to improve productivity by 10%, the next question should be "What is the deadline?" Do we need to reach the target in six months, nine months or a year?

The term "continuous improvement" infers that our efforts to reduce cost, improve quality and reduce cycle time will be unending. While this is true, specific timeframes must be defined. Targets combined with timeframe are the basic two ingredients for a performance measure.

As recommended above, senior management has the responsibility of defining initial timeframe deadlines for continuous improvement. The same three factors of current financial results, competitive position

and strategy should be considered when defining the timeframe for a targeted improvement. Beyond the first year, employees should be more actively involved in recommending timeframes for their targeted improvements of departmental activities and business processes.

Training

The final 'T' is training. Management and employees alike will need training to successfully act upon the activity information to achieve the targets in the required timeframe. This book addresses the training issue in three distinct ways. First, comes training on ABM and on the four basic ABM analysis techniques:

- Value Analysis
- Primary Analysis
- Business Process Analysis
- Benchmarking

Applying these four techniques to ABM information is both practical and powerful. Each of the four techniques are discussed beginning on page 55.

The second method of training is derived in the Five Steps of the Continuous Improvement chapters in this book. Each of the Five Steps require employees to combine their activity information with new or pre-existing techniques in problem solving, such as Cause-and-Effect Diagramming, "Five Why's" and Pareto Analysis.

Finally, this book provides an appendix of three case study examples to provide you practical training examples. Refer to the appendices at any time to walk through the Five Step Continuous Improvement Process for (1) improving the productivity of a department; (2) improving the productivity of a Business Process; and (3) innovating a business process.

Let's begin the training. Proceed to page 55 to learn more about Value Analysis.

 **Notes**

Value Analysis

Does your organization have any waste? How much waste does your organization contain? How much money is spent on needless or inefficient activities? Is waste 5%, 40%, or even 75% of your total costs? Inherently you recognize your company contains some waste and opportunities for improvement.

Value Analysis

Before ABM, most organizations talked or joked about waste. When asked to point to waste, managers would point to the waste related to products, such as material scrap. Before ABM, making waste visible to every employee was impossible.

If you were challenged to enhance the value added by the Receiving Department using the traditional view, you would find it difficult, if not impossible to do. The ABM view supports value enhancement.

In the absence of ABM information, managers are inappropriately eliminating the worker and not the work. For example, if you lay off a worker who expedites delinquent orders, without solving the root cause for rushing the order, the cost will only return in a future time period as overtime, a temporary or as another employee with a new job title. Without a relevant information system, managers take a shotgun approach to cost-cutting. Symptoms of this frustration are across-the-board cuts of 10%, freezing travel expenses or the ever-popular early retirement program. Senior management of companies all over the world are saying "there has got to be a better way to identify value and eliminate waste." There is. With ABM, organizations now have an easy tool for making waste visible to every level of employee. This technique is called Value Analysis.

Value analysis is the process of analyzing every activity within a department or business process to determine its contribution to meeting customer expectations. The object of Value Analysis is to optimize those activities which add value and minimize or eliminate non-value added activities.

Value Not Visible

Salaries	$545,000
Supplies	88,000
Depreciation	186,000
Space	51,000
All Other	74,000
Total Cost	$944,000

Receiving Department
Traditional View

Value Visible

Receive Material	$291,470
Move Material	302,940
Expedite Material	157,350
Manage Employees	138,140
Do Admin. Tasks	54,100
Total	$944,000

Receiving Department
ABM View

Value Analysis is not a new form of the Scarlet Letter, where people walk around with a "V" or "NV" on their forehead. Activities are non-value, not the people who perform them.

Value Analysis

A Value Added Activity is..

*An Activity **required** to meet external customer requirements*

*An Activity **required** by the Government or other regulatory agencies*

An Activity that modifies or enhances the Raw Materials of our product

An Activity that if we do more of, the customer might pay more for our product or service

An Activity which is a critical step that cannot be eliminated in a business process

An Activity performed to resolve or eliminate quality problems

An Activity performed due to a request or expectation of a satisfied customer

An Activity that produces a valuable output

An Activity, if time permitted, you would like to do more of

What is Value Added?

Webster's dictionary defines the word value as "That for which something is regarded as useful or desirable."

In their book *Dynamic Manufacturing*, Hayes, Wheelwright, and Clark state that "Value is defined by the customer". The notion is simple: any activity that does not produce added value for the customer is waste. Ford Motor Company agrees with this philosophy and instructs employees that "the voice of the customer determines value."

An increasingly popular value definition comes from companies installing Total Quality Management (TQM). Any activity performed to be in conformance with good manufacturing practices, customer specifications, or external regulations is value added. Conversely, any activity performed due to nonconformance is non-value added.

The Just-in-Time definition of value is very succinct. Any activity that touches the product is value added. Any activity that does not touch the product is non-value added. Activities such as Issue Purchase Order, Develop Marketing Plan, and Complete IRS Tax Reports using this definition are non-value added. The benefit of the JIT definition is that it is simple and easy to apply. The liability is that 90 percent of the company's activities are typically classified as non-value added. This is not common sense and is too overwhelming for analysis.

So which definition should you use? The answer lies in your organization strategic goals and objectives. No matter which definition your organization selects, remember that it should "mirror" the strategic goals and culture of your organization.

Team Exercise:

Which definitions on pages 56 and 57 best describe value and non-value to you and your company? Choose one or create your own.

_____

_____

_____

_____

What is Non-Value Added?

So why do non-value added activities exist? You don't necessarily want to "Rework Material", "Expedite Order", or "Wait for Repair". As the organization grows, processes break down and are patched for use, thereby making them complex. When errors take place, additional controls are put in place to review outputs rather than change the activity. In other words, "Inspect-in the Quality" instead of "Build-in the Quality". Even when the activity or business process is corrected, the controls often remain. Employees seldom talk to the customers of their output and hence do not clearly understand their requirements. Too much time is spent on internal maintenance of activities (such as coordinating, expediting, record keeping) instead of on redesigning the process to be mistakeproof.

When eliminating a Non-Value Added Activity, the C.I. Team must be very creative in coming up with solutions. The C.I. Team should not be constrained by current culture, personalities, or environment.

Typical Non-Value Activities	Solution
Rework Product	Can be eliminated only by removing the causes of the error.
Move Material	Can be minimized by combining operations, moving activities closer together, and by reducing inventory.
Wait for Repair	Can be minimized by performing preventative maintenance.
·Expedite Order	Can be reduced only by identifying and eliminating the root causes of customer requested expedites.
Count Inventory	Can be eliminated by changes in policies and procedures coupled with cycle counting verifications of accuracy.

A Non-Value Added Activity is...

An Activity that can be eliminated without impacting the form, fit, or function of the product

An Activity that begins with "Re" (i.e., Rework)

An Activity which results in "Waste" and adds no value to our product or service

An Activity performed due to inefficiency in the process upstream

An Activity which is duplicated in another department or adds unnecessary steps to the business process

An Activity performed to monitor quality problems

An Activity performed due to a request from an unhappy/ unsatisfied customer

An Activity that produces an unnecessary or unwanted output

An Activity, if given the option, you would prefer to do less of

Value Analysis

An organization typically finds 30-40% of its total cost is spent performing Non-Value Added Activities.

It is easier to eliminate than redeploy. Redeployment requires you to be <u>creative.</u>

 **Great Idea!**

Develop plans to grow your company 5% per year for the next five years without adding resources. The resources currently consumed by non-value activities will be needed to fund the 5% growth of all value activities.

What do you do with waste?

Before an organization begins defining and eliminating the root cause of non-value added activities, an important issue must be addressed and resolved: What will we do with the people and other resources that are no longer needed after the root causes of a non-value added activity are eliminated. Employees will not work themselves out of a job. Employees want and need to know what will be done with the resources (people, space, machines) consumed by non-value added activities. Senior management has two options.

(1) Eliminate the resources, or (2) Redeploy the resources.

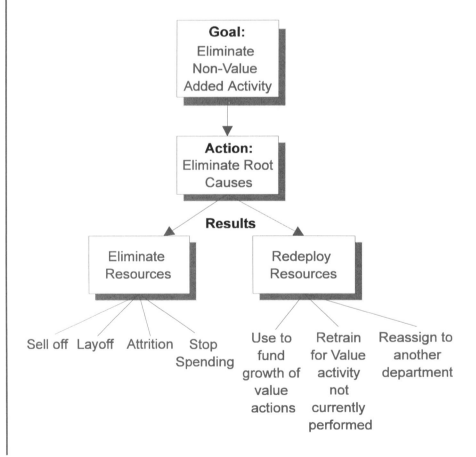

Team Exercises

Listed below are the activities for the Receiving Department. Each activity has been classified as Value or Non-value added.

Activity	Value $	Non-Value $	Total
Receive Material	$291,470		$291,470
Move Material		$302,940	$302,940
Expedite Material		$157,350	$157,350
Manage Employee	$138,140		$138,140
Do Admin Tasks	$54,100		$54,100
Total	$483,710	$460,290	$944,000
	51%	**49%**	**100%**

To calculate the Value Added percentage of 51%, divide the Value Added Total Cost ($483,710) by the Total Departmental Cost ($944,000). This calculation is repeated for the Non-Value Added percentage.

1) Do you agree with the value classifications in the example above? Why or why not?

2) Do you expect to find more than or less than 50% value in your entire company? Discuss the reasons for your response.

What do you think?

Employees are most often the best judge when it comes to classifying their activities as value or non-value.

List below the activities in your own department and their cost.

(1)　Classify each activity as value or non-value. What percentage of your department's cost is value added?

Activity	Value $	Non-Value $	Total
Total	$	$	$
	%	%	**100%**

(2)　List and discuss the reasons for your classifications.

_____

_____

_____

_____

_____

_____

 # Helpful Hints

■   Keep your definition of Value and Non-Value Added simple.

■   Let employees classified their own Activities as Value or Non-Value Added.

■   Optimize Activities that add Value. Minimize or eliminate Activities that do not add Value.

■   Ask yourself, Can the Value-added activities be done at a lower cost?

■   Can the Value Added Activity can be done in a shorter cycle time?

■   How can the Non-Value added activities be eliminated? If they cannot, can they be minimized?

 **Notes**

A large medical products distributor found that 50% of a sales representative's time was spent "Preparing Reports". A pharmaceutical firm found that one of their Top 10 most expensive activities was "Attend Meetings". A high tech firm found 30% of their design engineering costs were spent performing "Administrative Tasks", not "Designing New Products". Every well managed company is busy. The question is... "Doing what?"

Primary Analysis

To support Continuous Improvement, many organizations will classify activities as being either value or non-value added. Less controversial, yet equally beneficial, is the characterization of activities as being either Primary or Secondary.

Primary Activities contribute directly to the central mission of the department or organization. For example, the primary activities for a Sales department would be "Make Sales Presentation", "Take Order", or "Expedite Order". Typically, the output of a primary activity leaves the department or cost center.

Secondary Activities support an organization's primary activities. They are administrative in nature and occur in almost every department. Typical Secondary Activities are: Manage Employees, Train Employees, Attend Meetings, and Do Administrative Tasks.

Primary vs. Secondary Analysis often exposes that an organization is spending too much time and cost on administrative activities. Managers typically spend fifty percent of their time writing, reading, and attending meetings. Sixty percent of all clerical work is spent on checking, filing and retrieving information.

Primary Analysis often reveals an organization is spending too much time and cost on Administrative Activities (i.e., Red Tape).

> *Your goal should be to have a 90/10 ratio between your Primary and Secondary activity percentages.*

Primary Analysis

A typical Primary vs. Secondary Analysis reveals approximately 80% of an organization's resources are spent on primary activities and 20% on secondary. Your goal should be a 90/10 ratio. A high secondary percentage is symptomatic of excessive bureaucracy and inappropriate spans of control.

A secondary percentage greater than 10% is symptomatic of excessive bureaucracy and inappropriate spans of control.

An organization with seven to ten layers of management typically finds 20% of their Activity Cost is Secondary. Best practice is 4 to 5 layers and 10% Secondary cost.

An organization with four to five employees per supervisor typically find 20% of their Activity Cost is Secondary. Best practice is 12 to 15 people per supervisor.

To reduce resources being spent on Secondary Activities, identify the following:

- Unnecessary checks and balances
- Items requiring more than one signature
- Multiple copies being stored
- Unnecessary written correspondence
- Outdated organizational policy or procedures
- Inappropriate amount of employee training

Team Exercises

Listed below are the activities for the Receiving Department. Each activity has been classified as primary or secondary.

To calculate the Primary percentage of 80%, divide Primary Cost ($751,760) by the Total Cost ($944,000). This calculation is repeated for the Secondary percentage.

Activity	Primary $	Secondary $	Total
Receive Material	$291,470		$291,470
Move Material	$302,940		$302,940
Expedite Material	$157,350		$157,350
Manage Employees		$138,140	$138,140
Do Admin Task		$54,100	$54,100
Total	**$751,760**	**$192,240**	**$944,000**
	80%	**20%**	**100%**

1) Do you agree with the primary and secondary classifications? Why or why not?

2) Do you expect to find more than or less than 20% secondary cost in your entire company? Discuss the reasons for your response.

So what happened in those companies previously mentioned on page 63?

In the medical products company, many sales representative reports and paperwork were eliminated and sales territorial boundaries were reduced to minimize the secondary Activity, "Travel to Customer."

The high tech firm discovered $40,000 a year Engineers doing secondary activities previously performed by a laid off clerk who had been paid $20,000 per year. An administrative pool of clerks was added to support all administrative departments including Engineering.

The pharmaceutical firm implemented procedures to reduce the frequency and length of meetings in all functions by putting a basketball-sized time clock in each meeting room.

Primary Analysis

What do you think?

Employees are most often the best judge when it comes to classifying activities as primary or secondary.

1) Write below a one or two sentence description of the purpose or mission of your department:

_____

_____

_____

2) List below the activities in your own department and their cost. Classify each activity as primary or secondary. What percentage of your department's cost is secondary?

Activity	Primary $	Secondary $	Total
Total	$	$	$
	%	%	100%

3) List and discuss reasons why secondary costs are too high or too low.

_____

_____

_____

 **Notes**

Business Process Analysis

Ford Motor Company reduced its Accounts Payable Process 20% by a change in procedures: "Pay when we receive the product, not when we get the bill." Mutual Benefit Life improved their Insurance Claim Process from 25 days to just 2 days by a change in thinking: "Most claims are similar and can be handled by one person, not five or six." How did these and numerous other companies around the world obtain such radical improvements? By implementing an innovative new Continuous Improvement tool called Business Process Re-engineering.

Business Process Analysis

Know your flow. This is a simple phrase that describes business process analysis. A business process is a series of Activities typically performed by different departments and functions.

Business Process Analysis encourages you to ask, "Are we working together efficiently to satisfy our customer's needs?" Business Process Analysis begins with identifying a company's business processes. A Business Process is a collection of related activities operating under a set of procedures to accomplish a specific objective. Most organizations have 10 to 15 significant business processes. Examples include: Process a Customer Order, Procure Raw Materials, Design a New Product, or Budgeting. The activities of a process are related because a specific event triggers the first activity to occur which, in turn, triggers another activity which, in turn, triggers another, and so forth.

A great business process can be described as going to Disneyworld and not having to stand in line.

Business processes transcend the standard departmental boundaries of an organization, forcing employees to realize that their customer is not the person who buys the final product... it is more often the next department. The input of an activity is, more often than not, the output of

Business Process Analysis

an Activity in another department. For example, a customer call (input) triggers the Sales Activity "Take Order". The output of "Take Order" is the input that triggers the Planning Activity of "Schedule Order".

Employees begin to realize the performance of their Activity, in terms of cost, time and quality, has affects on departments downstream in the process. For example, workloads of many Activities in the procurement process might be the result of a purchasing department whose performance measure is to keep the purchase price of raw materials at a minimum. Because of this goal, the purchasing department might sacrifice the quality of raw materials for a lower price. In the long run, the overall company suffers because of the additional Activities incurred to correct and deal with the poor quality (i.e., Inspect Raw Materials, Process Scrap, Return Raw Materials, etc.).

Several business processes exist in your company. Most organizations focus solely on the production process, spending millions of dollars to improve it. Unfortunately, few organizations spend time or money focusing on improving business processes that support the manufacturing process (i.e., Sales Order, Procurement, etc.). What most organizations don't realize are that customers are five times more likely to turn to the competition, even if they are the "product leader", should there be inefficiencies in the support processes.

Five Steps to Business Process Analysis

Step 1: Select a Business Process

There are several factors to consider when selecting a business process for improvement. Analyze Business Processes...

...which consume a majority of the organization's resources.
...which are key to customer satisfaction.
...which have the largest amount of Non-Value.
...which have an exceptionally long cycle time.
...which have an inconsistent output.

Steps To Business Process Analysis

1. Select a Business Process

2. Identify purpose of the Process

3. Define Process Boundaries

4. Map the "As Is" Process

5. Determine Process Innovation or Improvement

An ABM information system provides reports to C.I. Teams, such as the example at the bottom of this page. ABM business process reports provide important information to assist your Business Process Analysis. Ranking the gross cost and evaluating the Non-Value Added percentage for each process will help you in selecting a process to improve or innovate. The Procurement Process below is a terrific target for improvement with its 43% Non-Value.

The ABM report will also provide your C.I. Team a starting point for Step 2 of Business Process Analysis: Mapping the Process. Every Activity listed in the report will need to be mapped into the process flowchart. The report also provides important workload data. The output quantity of each Activity can be added to the map to expose bottlenecks, constraints, duplication, and excess capacity.

Note that three of the Receiving Department's Activities are part of the Procurement Process report below.

Who maps the process? You must involve the people involved in the daily operations of the process.

ABM Procurement Process Report

ACTIVITIES	TOTAL COST	VALUE	NON-VALUE	DEPARTMENT	OUTPUT QTY.	COST PER OUTPUT
Run MRP	$700,000	$700,000	$0	Planning	100	$7,000
Issue Requisition	$145,000	$145,000	$0	Planning	2,200	$66
Issue Purchase Order	$250,000	$250,000	$0	Purchasing	1,800	$139
Handle Vendor Problem	$140,000	$0	$140,000	Purchasing	450	$311
Expedite Purchase Order	$145,000	$0	$145,000	Purchasing	440	$330
Certify Vendors	$175,000	$175,000	$0	Purchasing	12	$14,583
Receive Material	$291,470	$291,470	$0	Receiving	2,500	$117
Move Material	$302,940	$0	$302,940	Receiving	11,000	$28
Expedite Material	$157,350	$0	$157,350	Receiving	1,250	$126
Inspect Material	$225,000	$0	$225,000	Quality	2,500	$90
Expedite Material	$80,000	$0	$80,000	Quality	500	$160
Reject Material	$90,000	$0	$90,000	Quality	400	$225
Certify Vendor	$185,000	$185,000	$0	Quality	15	$12,333
Return Goods to Vendor	$60,000	$0	$60,000	Quality	375	$160
Pay Vendor Invoice	$205,000	$205,000	$0	Accounting	1,500	$137
Contact Vendor	$72,000	$0	$72,000	Accounting	250	$288
Issue Debit Memo	$65,000	$0	$65,000	Accounting	375	$173
Store Material	$102,000	$0	$102,000	Warehouse	1,800	$57
Cycle Count Inventory	$40,150	$0	$40,150	Warehouse	2,500	$16
TOTAL COST	**$3,430,910**	**$1,951,470**	**$1,479,440**			
TOTAL PERCENT	**100%**	**57%**	**43%**			

Business Process Analysis

Ten Typical Processes

Process Name	Sample Activity from the Process
Marketing	Do Market Research
	Advertise Product
Sales Order	Process Sales order
	Ship Customer Order
	Handle Customer Complaints
Procurement	Issue Purchase Order
	Receive materials
	Inspect Raw Materials
Manufacturing	Stamp Part
	Move Material
	Setup Machine
Product Design	Design Prototype
	Issue Engin. Change Notice
Compliance	Comply with OSHA
	Count Inventory
Business Planning	Develop Strategic Plan
	Develop Budget
	Forecast Sales
People	Hire New Employees
	Process Payroll
General Management	Close Monthly Books
	Promote Company Goodwill
Facilities	Perform Preventative Maint.
	Do Housekeeping
	Handle Waste Water Treatment

Step 2: Identify the purpose of the Business Process

Make sure the entire group understands the purpose of the process to the organization and to the final customer. The Procurement process, for example, is responsible for procuring raw materials for manufacturing. Manufacturing is, therefore, the customer of the Procurement process.

Step 3: Establish Business Process boundaries.

Business Process boundaries are the inputs and outputs that signal the beginning and completion of the process. For the Procurement Process, the boundaries might be a Customer Order, which initiates the first Activity "Run MRP", and a Vendor Check, signalling the completion of the process.

Step 4: Map the "As Is" Process

Mapping or flowcharting an existing business process is key to process improvement. By using simple flowcharting symbols and lines, an existing process is identified, setting the stage for process improvement or innovation.

As shown in the example, by linking the input(s) and output(s) of Activities, the workflow of the process is established. Establishing an accurate workflow of a process is the key to process improvement.

Tools to map a process:

1) *Post-It™ notes or 3" x 5" cards on a large piece of Kraft paper*
- or -

2) *Flowcharting software. Many products are available, such as* ABC Flowcharter *from Micrographix*

Procurement Process Map

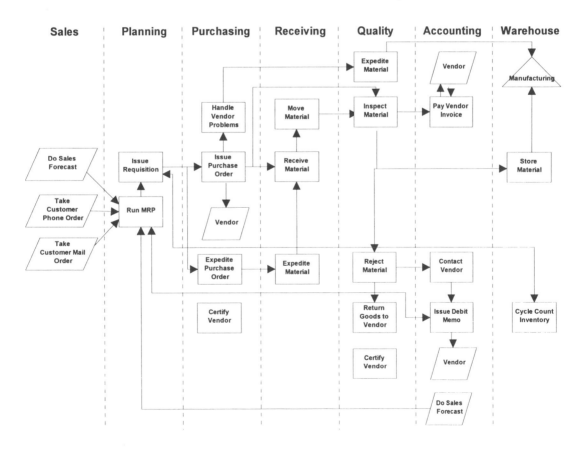

Business Process Analysis

Somebody must own each process, but someone rarely does at the onset.

Step 5 - Determine Process Innovation or Improvement

Once the business processes are established and mapped, the C.I. Team can either improve the process or innovate the process. Improvement and innovation require identification of process and work structure alternatives by comparing the existing "As Is" to an ideal "To Be" process.

Process Improvement
focuses on incremental improvements

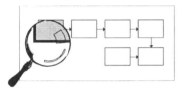

5-20% improvement

Process Improvement - Process Improvement is performing the "As Is" business process with moderate increased efficiency or effectiveness. Process improvement typically yields a 5-20% improvement in the cost, time and quality of the process. To improve a process, the C.I. Team should ask:

> Does the process structure support the customer requirements?
> Does every activity in the process add value?
> Are we duplicating work?
> How can we save time?
> Can we better utilize tools and equipment?
> Are there bottlenecks or constraints?

A simple way to begin process improvement is to identify the value added activities and identify projects to eliminate the non-value added activities. Streamline the process, eliminating unnecessary activities. For more radical changes, the C.I. Team should focus on Process Innovation.

Process Innovation
requires starting over

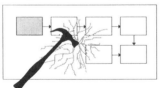

95% improvement

Process Innovation - Process Innovation is performing the business process in a "radically new way," eliminating both value and non-value added activities. The goal of Process Innovation is to have a 95% improvement in the process.

Process innovation requires re-engineering. Re-engineering has been loosely used to describe almost every sort of management improvement program under the sun. Therefore, let's start with a formal definition of reengineering to start our innovation:

"Reengineering is the radical redesign of strategic value-added business processes — and the systems, policies and organizational structures that support them — to optimize activity work flows and productivity in an organization."

Not all processes are candidates for innovation and re-engineering. In fact, most organizations can rarely deal with more than one or two re-engineering projects per year. Strategically important processes should be the target for initial innovation efforts — processes that are central to the success of the company. Your company would be in complete disarray if all processes were re-engineered in a 12-18 month span. A more practical approach is to improve most processes and innovate only a select few.

When innovating a process, start with a clean sheet of paper. Brainstorm a "To Be" process map. Consider technology and human implications. Implementing a new technology can be the basis for significantly innovating a business process.

Business Process Analysis will provide very valuable information to support your Continuous Improvement efforts, whether they be targeted towards…

Before innovating a business process, visit a benchmarking partner to view their best practice.

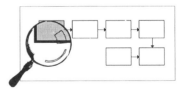 **Process Improvement**

- or -

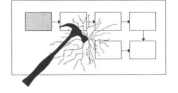 **Process Innovation**

Team Exercises

1)   List examples of companies you enjoy doing business with:

_____

_____

_____

_____

_____

_____

_____

2)   Is their secret a simple mistake-proof process? If so, how?
       Example: Doing business with Lands End catalog company.

_____

_____

_____

_____

_____

_____

3)   What process would you recommend mapping? Why?

_____

_____

_____

_____

_____

_____

_____

_____

_____

_____

 **Notes**

Benchmarking

In the late 1970's a team of top Xerox executives began visiting their competition in Japan. Xerox knew the Japanese were able to produce a copier for somewhat less, but Xerox felt comfortable the gaps were not enormous. After all, Xerox was experiencing a 7 to 8 percent productivity improvement per year, while most American companies were improving by only 2 or 3 percent. But, what Xerox found was that the Japanese were able to carry six to eight times less inventory. Quality of incoming raw materials parts were at 99.5%, compared to Xerox's 95%. Overhead rates for the Japanese was .6 per direct labor hour, while Xerox had an overhead rate of 1.3. Xerox found that the Japanese were not 50% better, they were close to 100% better in almost every category.

In light of these findings, Xerox embarked on a new Continuous Improvement Process of measuring their products, services, and practices against their toughest competitors and renowned leaders in the world. Xerox would first identify which company was the best at performing a certain operation (activity) and then set that as the company goal for improvement. What Xerox was doing was Benchmarking their activities and business processes.

Benchmarking

Benchmarking is the process of continually searching for the best methods, practices and procedures for an activity or business process and adopting or adapting these features to become the "best of the best." A "benchmark" is the leader in an activity or business process. It serves as a reference point for setting an organization's internal targets or goals.

Benchmarking can provide an organization a blueprint for leaping ahead of its competitors. Competitive advantage often occurs by improving administrative processes such as procurement or customer support, not through improvements or innovations in a company's most visible functional area, such as manufacturing. With activities serving as the basis for benchmarking, a manufacturer's billing process can be readily compared to a world class billing process of a service organization.

Companies often blindly set internal targets or goals. Until you benchmark your activities against the best, you'll never know how good you can be or should be. ABM provides an excellent tool for setting internal targets or goals.

Benchmarking

If your organization is not benchmarking to global best practices of activities and processes within the next five years, you may find yourself shadow boxing with last place.

Four Steps to Benchmarking

Step 1 - Select an Activity or Business Process to Benchmark

There are several factors to consider when selecting an Activity or Process to benchmark. First, select an Activity or Business Process that consumes significant costs. Benchmarking will take an investment in your time and potentially travel expenses. Therefore, the Activity or Business Process you select to benchmark should have the potential for significant savings or create a competitive advantage.

Do not Benchmark Non-Value Added Activities or Waste

Don't spend time benchmarking Waste or Non-Value Added Activities. When it comes to Activities such as Re-Work Product, Inspect Work-In-Progress, or Resolve Customer Complaints, common sense should lead us to eliminate the Activity, not improve the Activity through benchmarking. Define and eliminate the root causes of Non-Value. As Michael Hammer recommends: "Don't automate...Obliterate."

Understand Yourself Before Understanding Others

You cannot effectively benchmark unless you first document your own Activities, Outputs and Activity Cost. Describe your Activities as simple verb + noun combinations. Define an Output and Output Measure for each Activity.

For example:

Activity	Output	Output Measure	Gross Activity Cost	Output Quantity	Cost per Output
Take Order	An Order	Number of Orders	$150,000	3,000	$50.00
Setup Machine	A Setup	Number of Setups	$200,000	1,000	$200.00

Steps To Benchmarking

1. Select an Activity or Process to Benchmark

2. Select a Benchmarking Partner

3. Contact the Benchmark Partner

4. Act on the Benchmarking information

Rules for Benchmarking

#1 - *Understand yourself before understanding others*
#2- *Use a common activity output measure*
#3- *Use the correct level of detail*
#4- *Use a common cost structure*
#5- *Benchmark outside your industry*
#6- *Use common sense when benchmarking*

You will want to benchmark the Cost per Output with a benchmarking partner who:

1)   Uses the same output measure as you, and

2)   Has a significantly lower Cost per Output than you.

Use the Correct Level of Detail

Perform your Activity Analysis at the correct level of detail. There is very little benchmarking value in understanding your Activities and processes in minute detail. Document the 5 to 10 significant Activities per department. Then map those Activities into your 10 to 15 high level Business Processes. A detailed flowchart of a Sales Order Process with 100 steps, tasks, and decision points will only scare your benchmarking partner. An Activity Map, such as displayed on page 73, best serves the benchmarking discussion.

Use A Common Activity Output Measure

When benchmarking an Activity with another organization, make sure you share a common output measure. For example, for the Activity "Take Order", make sure you and your benchmarking partner are using the same output measure. Your analysis will be invalid if your output measure is "Number of Sales Orders", While your benchmarking partner uses "Number of Lines per Sales Order".

Use a Common Cost Structure

When benchmarking Activity Cost, make sure the categories of resources traced to the Activity are similar to your benchmarking partners. For example, if you traced the costs of building space to each Activity, but your benchmarking partner overlooked this resource, the Activity Cost comparison is invalid.

When benchmarking, compare not only the total cost of an Activity, but also the list of resources consumed.

Benchmarking

To illustrate the importance of a common language for benchmarking, James Blatt of Edison Brothers Stores, Inc. in St. Louis, recently wrote the following letter to the editor of CFO Magazine. His letter was in reference to an article on benchmarking of finance and accounting.

"The charts in the 'Anatomy of Finance' illustrate one of the fundamental problems with benchmarking - how to achieve an apples-to-apples comparison. For example, the cost per paycheck for the payroll function at Digital Equipment Corporation is reported at $1.04. The next line gives the number of paychecks issued per Full Time Equivalent employee - 108,000. This implies that the cost of a Full Time Equivalent employee is in excess of $112,320 per year ($1.04 x 108,000). Even with the escalating cost of fringe benefits, this appears high. Either there is something else in the cost of a paycheck besides labor, or we have a dramatically underpaid staff in our payroll department."

Digital Equipment Corporation included all of the resources consumed in producing a payroll check - not just the salary and fringes of the payroll department employees. When benchmarking, compare not only the total cost of an Activity, but also the list of resource costs consumed. In most organizations, the Activity "Issue Paycheck" consumes resources such as people, floor space, computers, software, supplies, telephones and other miscellaneous costs.

Step 2 - Select a Benchmarking Partner

There are three main types of Benchmarking. Each method yields a different percentage of improvement for the Activity or Business Process, so select the method that best fits your goals.

Internal Benchmarking - This is the process of benchmarking within your own organization. This includes benchmarking with another department, functional area, location, division, or plant site.

> ## Internal Benchmarking
> ### Yields a 10% improvement

Competitor Benchmarking - This is the process of benchmarking with a competitor. This is typically the most difficult of the benchmarking methods for obvious reasons. Competitors will likely shy away from providing you competitive secrets.

> ## Competitive Benchmarking
> ### Yields a 20% improvement

Best in Class Benchmarking - This is the process of benchmarking outside your industry with the "best in class". For example, when Texas Instruments Defense Systems wanted to learn how to ship products within 24 hours at 99.9% accuracy, they benchmarked with Mary Kay Cosmetics.

> ## Best in Class Benchmarking
> ### Yields a 35% improvement

In most instances, you will find it easier to benchmark with noncompetitors than competitors. Activities will serve as the common language. Southwest Airlines, for example, benchmarked their aircraft gate turnaround process (15-20 minutes), the best in the airline industry, to a race car refueling process of an Indianapolis 500 pit crew (15-20 seconds). Each organization understood their activities and processes.

There are several resources available when investigating and selecting a benchmarking partner:

- ■ Magazines or Other General Publications
- ■ Professional Organizations
- ■ Libraries and Universities
- ■ Seminars
- ■ Benchmarking Clearinghouse
- ■ ICMS, Inc.

Benchmarking

Organizations must use common sense and select only significant activities and processes to benchmark.

Use Common Sense when Benchmarking

Everywhere is within walking distance if you have the time. But how much time do you realistically have to benchmark and improve the performance of your activities, business processes and products? The answer is that you don't have as much time as you think. Competition is either breathing down your neck or in front speeding away. As a result, organizations must use common sense and select only significant activities and processes to benchmark. Choose time consuming processes that are strategically important such as New Product Development. Or target activities that consume significant resource costs.

In addition, don't think that you must travel to benchmark. Stay home and benchmark activity and business processes using your own common sense. While grocery shopping with my spouse recently, I picked up a can of peas priced at $2.35. The price seemed high. I asked myself, "I wonder how much non-value added activity costs are in the price of the product?" My spouse returned me to my senses stating, "It costs too much. Put it back." In other words, my spouse was applying Common Sense Benchmarking. If the cost per output seems to be too high, then it probably is!

When speaking to the Benchmarking Partner, remember:

...Ask for information you would provide under the same circumstances.
...Be honest and complete with all information provided.
...Convey to the benchmarking expert that the information they provide is strictly confidential.

Step 3 - Contact the Benchmarking Partner

Before visiting with the benchmarking partner, correspond with them via phone, fax or mail. Both organizations should agree to the following:

1) What activity and/or business process will each organization share with the other partner? For benchmarking to work, both partners must be willing to share with the other any activity or process they do well and is of interest to the other partner.

2) Agree to a meeting site, agenda and list of participants. Participants in the meeting should be the people who actually do the activities being benchmarked.

Step 4 - Act upon Benchmarking Information

Implement the benchmarking ideas and information obtained in the benchmarking visit. The C.I. Team will need to identify policy and procedure changes necessary for implementation along with any additional resource requirements.

To effectively plan and confirm that implementing the benchmark ideas are appropriate and achievable, the department impacted should review their activity accounting worksheet. For example, if you visited a company that does "Receive Material" for $10.00 per receipt, make sure you learned how to put together a resource cost plan that allows you to achieve the $10.00 benchmark. To achieve $10.00 per output in the example below would require significant elimination or redeployment of resources.

COST	TOTAL	Receive Material Primary/Value	Move Material Primary/Non-Value	Expedite Material Primary/Non-Value	Manage Employee Secondary/Value	Do Admin. Task Secondary/Value
Supplies	$88,000	$35,200	$15,000	$21,000	$6,240	$10,560
Depreciation	$186,000	$35,000	$110,000	$35,000	$3,000	$3,000
Salaries	$545,000	$179,850	$141,700	$81,750	$109,000	$32,700
Space	$51,000	$17,000	$17,000	$8,500	$5,100	$3,400
All Other	$74,000	$24,420	$19,240	$11,100	$14,800	$4,440
Total Cost	$944,000	$291,470	$302,940	$157,350	$138,140	$54,100
Output Measure Quantity		2,500	11,000	1,250	10	10
Output Measure		Receipts	Moves	Expedites	Employees	Employees
Cost per Output		$117	$28	$126	$13,814	$5,410

Benchmarking

Sources for Benchmarking data:

ICMS, Inc.

The Benchmarking
    Clearinghouse

Gunn Partners

A.T. Kearney

Institute of Management
    Accountants

Actual Benchmarks

Here are some actual activity benchmarks compiled in 1994 by a U.S. corporation during their Accounting Department continuous improvement process:

Accounting Department	Activity	Output Measure	Cost per Output	
			Average of Companies Called	Best Practice
Accounts Payable	Issue Checks	Number of Checks	$8.00	$1.00
Receivables	Issue Checks	Number of Checks	$16.00	$6.00
General Accounting	Process Expense Checks	Number of Expense Reports	$20.00	$2.00
Payroll	Issue Checks	Number of Checks	$6.00	$0.75

1) Which activity in your department would you recommend benchmarking? Why?

_____

_____

_____

2) Who do you recommend benchmarking against?

_____

_____

_____

3) Your benchmarking partners will want to know something you do well. What will you share?

_____

_____

_____

Helpful Hints

■ Get an active commitment to benchmarking from your senior management.

■ Develop an internal benchmarking expert to coordinate benchmarking projects.

■ Understand yourself before attempting to understand others. Know your activities and business processes in terms of cost, quality, and time.

■ Seek out the best practice. Benchmark outside your company and industry.

■ Don't spend time benchmarking waste or non-value added activities.

■ Be willing to share information with your benchmarking partner.

■ Benchmark at the correct level of detail. Activities and processes, not tasks or steps.

■ When benchmarking activity cost, verify the types of resources consumed by the activity are similar.

■ Act on benchmarking findings.

Notes

Team Exercise

1)   What Value Added Activity have you targeted for improvement?

    _____

    _____

    _____

2)   Which Non-Value Activity have you targeted for elimination or reduction? Why this one?

    _____

    _____

    _____

3)   What is your ratio of Primary versus Secondary Activity in your department? Is it over or under the 10% recommended level? Why?

    _____

    _____

    _____

4)   What Business Process have you recommended to map? Why? Do you recommend improvement or innovation? Should you benchmark?

    _____

    _____

    _____

Step 2: Identify Root Causes

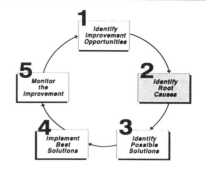

Meeting Notes

Attendees:
C.I. Team members

Objective:
To perform a "root cause" analysis

Meeting Time:
1 to 1 1/2 hours

Supplies:
- Overhead projector
- Pens
- Overhead of fishbone diagram
- Flipchart

Meeting Agenda

- Agree to meeting agenda and meeting length.

- Review and agree to the Activity or process that has been targeted in Step 1 for improvement or innovation.

- Review and discuss Root Cause analysis techniques.

- Perform Cause-and-Effect Analysis. Follow the Four Step approach:

    1. Draw a cause-and-effect diagram on a flipchart, stating problem as "head" of fish.
    2. Establish 4 or 5 root cause categories as "bones" of the fish.
    3. Brainstorm possible causes on each "bone" of the fish.
    4. Identify Root Cause.

- Review Appendices A, B & C as examples.

- Define "To Do's" for Step 3; identify possible solutions.

- Wrap-up.

Root Cause Analysis

Take a look at the pattern to the right. Find a perfect star. As you look for it, try to be aware of the search strategies you use.

How did you do? Did you find it? (If not, see the next page.) The point of the exercise is demonstrate that you need to have some idea of what you're looking for in order to find it. So the main question is: Did you define what you were looking for? Is it a five-pointed star? A Star of David? A seven-pointed sheriff's star? Is it a big star? A little star? Is it composed of both black and white triangles?

Your C.I. Team should have a well-defined activity or process opportunity before embarking upon finding an answer.

Cause-and-Effect Diagrams

A Cause-and-Effect Diagram, called a "Fishbone Diagram" because of its appearance, allows you to map out a list of root causes that cause an activity, process, stated problem or affect a desired outcome. A Cause-and-Effect Diagram typically has a large arrow pointing to a stated problem. Pointing to the larger arrow are branches representing the main categories of potential causes of the stated problem. For Activity Based Management purposes, *Causes* represent the reasons why an activity or process occurs. *Effect* represents the name of the activity or business process affected by the causes.

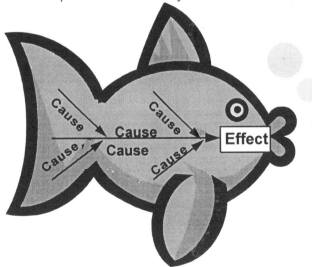

"For there are few things as useless - if not dangerous - as the right answer to the wrong question."
Peter E. Drucker
The Practice of Management

Root Cause Analysis

The Cause-and-Effect Diagram creates a structured method for generating causes and solutions to any stated activity improvement for use by the C.I. Team.

Four Steps to Cause-and-Effect Diagramming

Step 1 - Draw the Cause-and-Effect Diagram

On a flipchart, draw the Cause-and-Effect Diagram and write the improvement problem at the head of the fish. To demonstrate the technique, let's diagram a problem of "Bad Tasting Coffee."

Step 2 - Establish four or five root cause categories

Establishing four or five root cause categories will stimulate the team's thinking about root causes. The most common categories for the "bones" are: People, Procedure, Material, and Equipment. The "bones" of the fish can be labeled with any category title the C.I. Team feels will stimulate ideas. Smaller arrows, representing causes will be drawn off the four bones.

Steps To Cause-and-Effect Diagramming

1. Draw the Cause-and-Effect Diagram

2. Establish 4 or 5 root cause categories

3. Begin Brainstorming root causes

4. Identify Root Cause.

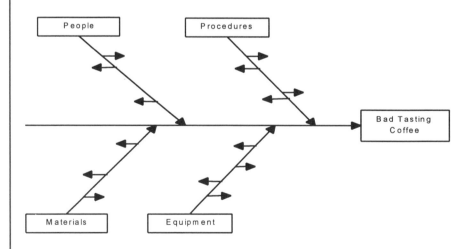

Step 3 - Begin brainstorming

*Brainstorm the possible causes on each "bone" of the fish. As the C.I. Team begins brainstorming, focus on one "bone" at a time. If an idea comes up that better fits in another category, don't debate the category, just write the idea down. The purpose of this step is to stimulate ideas, not to develop a list that is perfectly organized.

Generate as many ideas as possible for each branch of the diagram.

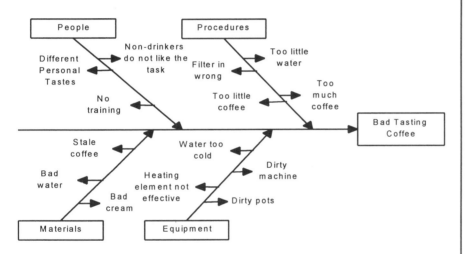

*Note: If you are unfamiliar with the brainstorming technique, read pages 105-107 of this book.

"Fishbone" Tips

- *Avoid criticizing ideas*
- *Build on the ideas of others*
- *Encourage wild ideas*

Root Cause Analysis

Step 4 - Identify Root Cause

After identifying the various causes in Step 3, there are two techniques to identify the Root Cause.

Option 1: Repeat Steps 1, 2 and 3 on the previous page for any cause listed on the cause-and-effect diagram. For example, you might create a fishbone diagram for the "Dirty Machine" cause.

The "root cause" is the primary cause of the activity. An activity may have many causes but only <u>one</u> root cause.

Option 2: Perform a Pareto analysis. A Pareto Chart is a useful tool to define the 20% of activity causes that result in 80% of the problem. As depicted below, note the tallest bar highlights that the cause, "Dirty Machine," represents the primary root cause for bad tasting coffee. The height of the bar indicates, on a scale of 0% to 100%, the percentage that each cause is considered influential to the problem. The C.I. Team should now focus on identifying possible solutions for the causes having the greatest influence on the stated problem. For this example, a solution for a dirty coffee machine should be the team's focus for the next chapter and Step 3: Identify Possible Solutions.

Bad Tasting Coffee has occurred 100 times. Of those 100 times:

Root Cause	Number of Occurrences
Dirty Machine	50
Too Little Water	25
Filter in Wrong	15
Stale Coffee	<u>10</u>
	100

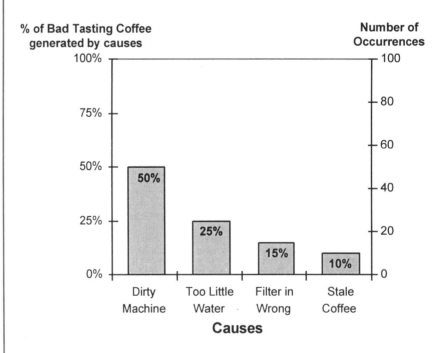

Exercise

Create a fishbone diagram for an activity in your department. Brainstorm the root causes and document them on the fishbone diagram below.

Idea
Select an activity or problem you have been complaining about.

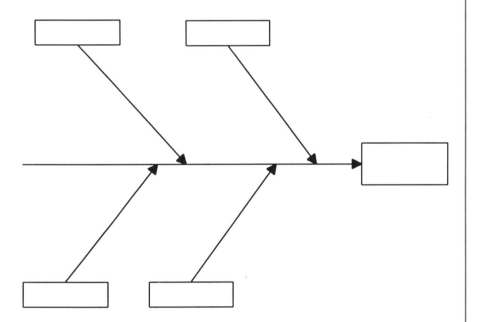

Root Cause Analysis

Shortcut

Root Cause Shortcut

The four steps outlined in this chapter represent a practical and thorough approach to defining activity and process root causes. In some cases, however, a C.I. Team may wish to shortcut the analysis because of time constraints or lack of data. If this is the case, we recommend using the Five Why's approach to define the root cause of an activity, process or opportunity.

For example, if "Perform Emergency Maintenance" is your most expensive non-value activity, your "Five Why's" analysis might go as follows:

Q:	Why do we do so much "Perform Emergency Maintenance?"
A:	Because we do not do preventive maintenance.

Q:	Why don't we do preventive maintenance?
A:	Because we don't schedule or plan preventive maintenance on our machinery.

Q:	Why don't we schedule preventive maintenance?
A:	We did in the past, but we don't today because we use that time for frequent changeovers of machines from one product to another.

Q:	Why are there so many changeovers that consume so much time?
A:	Because we often start a production run and then discover we are out of certain raw materials.

Q:	Why do we run out of raw material?
A:	Because our inventory system is 20 years old and very inaccurate.

The root cause of "Perform. Emergency Maintenance" is the outdated, inaccurate inventory system. Until the inventory system is improved, emergency maintenance will not likely diminish in cost or time requirements.

 **Team Exercise:**

Select an activity in your department. Do a "Five Why's" analysis.

Q: Why do we do _____?

A:

Q:

A:

Q:

A:

Q:

A:

Q:

A:

Chapter Summary

Cause-and-Effect Diagramming is used to list the factors thought to affect an activity, business process or stated problem by arranging causes on a "fishbone" diagram. The steps for creating and using a Cause-and-Effect are:

1. Draw the Cause-and-Effect diagram on a flipchart, stating the activity or problem at the "head" of the fish.

2. Establish four or five major categories of causes to stimulate the group to think about causes. Major categories of causes are typically People, Procedure, Material and Equipment. Causes are placed on the "bones" of the fish by major category.

3. The C.I. Team should brainstorm the possible causes on each "bone" of the fish. The organization of the branches is not as important as the generation of ideas.

4. The group should narrow down the list to the most probable root causes.

Everyone in the group should be encouraged to participate, and there should be no criticizing of ideas. The diagram should be large enough for the entire group to see it. If the diagram seems to be overloaded, or ideas are not grouped logically, separate diagrams should be created as needed. Finally, the group should narrow down the list, focusing on the most likely root causes, and circle them.

 **Notes**

Step 3: Identify Possible Solutions

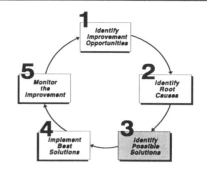

Meeting Notes

Attendees:
    C.I. Team members

Objective:
    Identify possible
    solutions to the "root
    causes" defined in
    Step 2

Meeting Time:
    1 to 1 1/2 hours

Supplies:
- Butcher paper
- Tape
- Pins
- 3 packages of 5x8 index cards (3 different colors)
- Pens
- Colored sticker dots
- Handout of Storyboarding or Brainstorming chapter

Meeting Agenda

- Agree to Meeting Agenda and Meeting Length.

- Review the results of the Step 2 Root Cause Analysis. Agree to the Root Cause to be Solved.

- Review and discuss the Storyboarding and Brainstorming techniques.

- Identify possible solutions using either:

Brainstorming
1. Define the problem
2. Generate possible solutions
3. Narrow the ideas

Storyboarding
1. Define the problem
2. Participants generate and record ideas
3. Ideas are posted on the wall
4. Ideas are grouped by common themes
5. Ideas are prioritized

- Review Appendices A, B & C for examples.

- Define "To Do's" for Step 4 - Implement Best Solutions.

- Wrap-up.

Brainstorming

Why does a professional photographer take hundreds of pictures when shooting a particular subject? For example, at my wedding last year, the photographer took over 600 pictures, but our final wedding album contained only 75 pictures. Your first response might be that my husband or I must blink a lot. But in truth, the photographer took many pictures due to changing situations, lighting, and mix of people attending, anticipating that only a few pictures would be good. The same goes for generating Continuous Improvement ideas. Get more ideas than you can use, because only a select few will likely work.

Brainstorming

Brainstorming is a creative technique used to generate ideas and solutions. Brainstorming, when focused on Activities, Processes, and Root Causes is a powerful tool to create terrific Continuous Improvement Action Plans.

Brainstorming taps the thinking power of an entire C.I. Team. Ideas generated by the entire C.I. Team will be much more numerous and creative than those of a single individual. But how can brainstorming help to determine the best solutions to improve Activities? Start with the assumption that employees are conscientious, aware of problems affecting the quality of their work, and have thought about solutions. Employees contain a wealth of good solutions, which are often overlooked by senior management.

The factory of the information age is the human mind. Yet the average person uses less than one-tenth of one percent of his brain power.

"Nothing is more dangerous than an idea when it is the only one you have."

Emile Chartier
Philosopher

Brainstorming

Steps To Brainstorming
1. Ready
2. Fire
3. Aim

Three Steps to Brainstorming

Ready, Fire, Aim. You won't shoot many ducks using this sequence, but you can brainstorm some great ideas to improve your activities!!!

Step 1 - "Ready" (Define the Problem)

Identify the problem before you create a solution. The best ideas start with a passion to solve a specific problem or find an answer to a burning issue or opportunity.

The C.I. Team should focus on the Root Cause defined in Step 2 of the C.I.P. Process. State the root cause in a clear and concise manner. For example:

> How can we improve the quality of incoming raw materials?
> How can we reduce the number of expedite orders?
> How can we reduce the cost of issuing a purchase order?

Defining the issue to focus on is critical. The world changed for ever when the first nomad stopped asking "How do we get to water?" and asked instead, "How can we get the water to us?"

Step 2 - "Fire" (Generate Possible Solutions)

The C.I. Team should now begin to brainstorm possible solutions for the problem. Try contributing ideas in turn. Begin with one person and going all the way around the group. The more diverse the group, the better the ideas. Use this technique at the beginning of a session to ensure all C.I. Team members participate. If a C.I. Team member can't think of anything to contribute, their response should be "Pass." The ideas of each team member should be written down. Avoid judgement.

Constant attention must be given to the basics of brainstorming, such as:

> "Is everyone thinking about the same problem?"
> "Are all ideas encouraged and accepted without criticism?"
> "Do all of the group members have an equal chance to participate?"

The C.I. Team should generate a large number of ideas. The C.I. Team should accept all of the ideas, even the silly and outrageous ones. At the end of the session, the C.I. Team should filter through all the ideas and select those the C.I. Team feels are good.
Remember: Choose an idea-inspiring location for your brainstorming session. Hold the meeting early in the day to get the best ideas.

Step 3 - "Aim" (Narrow the Ideas to One Solution)

Now it is time to take aim.

After the C.I. Team has generated a long list of ideas, the next step is to narrow the list. A simple way of doing this is to give each team member 5 votes. Vote on each idea. C.I. Team members can apply all 5 votes to one idea or allocate them over several. Remove those ideas which received one or no votes. Repeat this process until the list narrows and number of ideas become manageable.

Take this narrowed list to Step 4: *Implementing Best Solutions* (next chapter).

According to research conducted by Charles Thompson, the top 10 idea-generating times are when you are:

1) *Sitting on the toilet*
2) *Showering or shaving*
3) *Commuting to work*
4) *Falling asleep or waking up*
5) *In a boring meeting*
6) *Reading at leisure*
7) *Exercising*
8) *Waking in the middle of the night*
9) *Listening to a church sermon*
10) *Performing manual labor*

Brainstorming

 **Exercise:**

Hold a brainstorming session in your department to try out the technique. Ask someone to be the leader of the session. Brainstorm the reasons why employees prefer home over work.

List ideas why:

1) _____

2) _____

3) _____

4) _____

5) _____

6) _____

7) _____

8) _____

9) _____

10) _____

Do any of the reasons have anything to do with the Activities or Root Causes of waste in your department?

 **Notes**

Storyboarding

Take a look around the room and find five things that are red.

With a "red" mind set, you'll find that red jumps right out at you: a red book on the table, a red chair in the room, red in the painting on the wall, and so on. Similarly, whenever you learn a new word, you hear it many times in the next few days. That's because people tend to find what they are looking for. It's all a matter of focusing your attention. Red represents all of the continuous improvement opportunities exposed by ABM.

STORYBOARDING

Storyboarding is a visualization tool used to assist the C.I. Team in generating a large number of ideas within a specified timeframe. Storyboarding was originally used by Walt Disney to assist in the production of cartoons. Disney used storyboarding to lay out cartoons.

Storyboarding is similar to brainstorming, but differs in that it produces organized, or categorized, groupings of ideas. Storyboarding also differs in that it allows for anonymous contribution of ideas. Storyboarding should, therefore, be used when dealing with a sensitive issue.

Don't overlook the obvious. Sometimes the most realistic and useful ideas are staring you right in the face.

Take, for example, the evolution of the bicycle. The first bicycle had both wheels the same size, but there was no drive train connecting them. The pedals were, instead, connected to the front wheel only. As time progressed, the front wheel was enlarged to increase speed. At one point, the front wheel got to be almost 5 feet in diameter and was considered unsafe. The solution to a better and safer bicycle came from the manufacturing line where the bicycles were built. Someone on the manufacturing line simply by suggesting using a drive chain to link the two wheels, optimized speed and safety.

Storyboarding is an excellent tool to avoid overlooking the obvious.

Storyboarding

Steps To Storyboarding
1. Define the problem
2. Participants generate and record ideas
3. Ideas are posted on the wall
4. Ideas are grouped by common themes
5. Ideas are prioritized

Benefits of Storyboarding:

- *Ideas are anonymous, which encourages frankness and reduces possible boss dominance.*

- *The C.I. Team's work is recorded on the wall, in an easy-to-understand format, providing an excellent summary of the results.*

- *If left up on the wall as a communication mechanism, it can show work in progress or work to be completed.*

Five Steps To Storyboarding

Step 1 - Define the Problem

The C.I. Team Leader or meeting facilitator posts the problem identified in the Step 2: Identify Root Cause session on a wall. The Root Cause is written on a 5" x 8" card or Post-It™ note. Examples might be: "Identify solutions to the root causes of the procurement process", or "Identify possible solutions to poor customer satisfaction".

Step 2 - Participants Generate and Record Ideas

The C.I. Team Leader gives each C.I. Team member ten 5" x 8" index cards and a marker. Each C.I. Team member generates solutions to the problem, recording each one on a card. Team members should print each idea clearly, keeping it to a single concise sentence or phrase.

Give the C.I. Team about ten minutes to silently generate ideas, giving when necessary, individuals additional cards as needed.

Step 3 - Ideas are Posted on the Wall

At the end of the allotted idea generation period (or sooner, if everyone is finished), the C.I. Team Leader collects the cards and posts them randomly on a wall of the room. Cards listing duplicate ideas are removed from the wall, leaving one to represent the idea.

Step 4 - Ideas are Grouped by Common Themes

The C.I. Team reviews all ideas that have been posted, and then begins to group them into similar categories. Colored 5" x 8" index cards are typically used as header cards above each grouping to denote its category of ideas. The C.I. Team Leader now leads a group discussion on each of the header cards. All participants are asked if there are ideas that should be added.

Step 5 - Ideas are Prioritized

The C.I. Team should prioritize or reduce the number of ideas, selecting those which best solve the stated problem. Each team member is given 5 colored sticker dots to affix to those cards felt to be most important. Dots represent everyone's vote. Allow them to affix the dots to the cards on the wall. It creates a fun experience. Also, the colored dots give you a visual picture of the vote. The cards with one or more dots then become the focus of future team efforts in Step 4: Implement Best Solutions (next chapter).

Storyboard Example

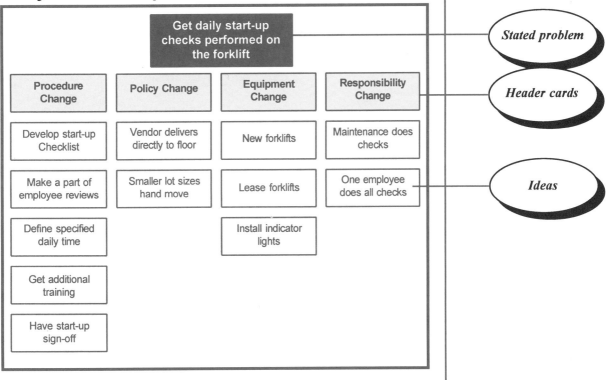

 **Helpful Hints**

Gather the storyboarding session supplies ahead of time to ensure that there will be enough for everyone at the session.

For each session, you should have the following items:

- Sheet of butcher paper (dark butcher paper usually works best) to hang on the wall
- A package of reusable putty, tape or pins for hanging the butcher paper on the wall
- Removable Magic tape for placing cards on the butcher paper
- Large colored card for posting the "problem" on the wall
- Ten colored 5" x 8" cards for each participant to write down their solutions to the problem
- Different colored 5" x 8" cards to denote categories of solutions, used as header cards above each grouping of ideas
- A marker for each participant
- Five round colored dot stickers for each participant to place on the cards to denote which ideas best solve the stated problem

Exercise:

Hold a storyboarding session in your department to try out the technique. Storyboard the reasons why previous continuous improvement or cost reduction initiatives have failed in your company.

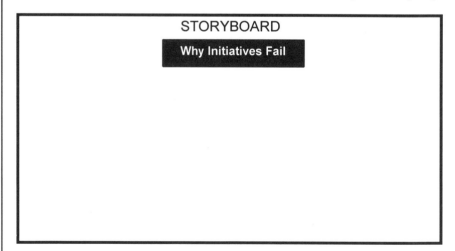

Apply what you learn to insure ABM does not fail.

 **Notes**

Step 4: Implement Best Solutions

Meeting Notes

Attendees:
    C.I. Team members

Objective:
    Develop a C.I. Plan

Meeting Time:
    1 to 2 hours

Supplies:
    - Action Plan forms
    - Steps 1-3 Notes

Meeting Agenda

■ Review Agenda and agree to meeting length.

■ Review and discuss the solutions developed in Step 3. Discuss what has been learned.

■ Develop a C.I. Plan using an approach of:
    1.   Identify key criteria
    2.   Select the best solution
    3.   Develop an Implementation Plan
    4.   Implement

■ Define "To Do's" for Step 4.

■ Review Appendices A, B & C for examples.

■ Set date for meeting with C.I. Committee or Senior Management to gain approval for the project plan.

■ Wrap-up.

Developing a Continuous Improvement Plan

How do you plan a trip? Do you arrive at the airport and request a ticket for any destination? Do you get into your car and just start driving? Do you board a bus not knowing where it is going? Generally, no. While you may overlook a detail or two, most people have a more comprehensive plan. How much money do they have to spend on the trip? Where will they go that is within the budget? What form of transportation is best to get there? Most people develop an itinerary containing specific points of interest, places to eat and shop, and other items key to make the trip successful. These same principles apply when developing and implementing a Continuous Improvement Plan.

Developing a Continuous Improvement Plan

If a giant jigsaw puzzle were approached in the fashion most managers approach the Continuous Improvement process, you would see puzzle pieces flying everywhere, many groups of two or three pieces fitting together, but nothing that resembles the complete puzzle. A disciplined approach that brings out the best of our past knowledge, the best of our creative talents, and the best of our analytical skills is required to develop a plan that will result in Continuous Improvement.

Steps To Implementing a C.I. Plan
1. Identify Key Criteria
2. Select the Best Solution
3. Develop an Implementation Plan
4. Implement

Weights do not have to be precise, but they should be relevant to the solution you wish to select.

Four Steps to Implementing a C.I. Plan

Step 1- Identify Key Criteria

Once the C.I. Team has developed a list of possible solutions, the next step is to select a solution for implementation. The first step in this process is to weigh all the possible solutions against a predetermined set of criteria or rules. The most useful tool in this process is a **Solution Rating Matrix.**

A Solution Rating Matrix allows the C.I. Team to compare/weigh the various solutions against a set of key criteria or rules. Some typical criteria to consider are:

■ **Ease of Implementation**
How easy would it be to implement this solution?

■ **Effectiveness of Solution**
How effective would the solution be in addressing the root cause and solving the problem?

■ **Probability of Success**
How likely is it that the solution itself could successfully be implemented?

■ **Resistance to Solution**
How much resistance might there be to implementing the solution?

■ **Cost**
How much will it cost to implement the solution?

Once the key criteria have been identified, the C.I. Team now needs to weigh each criteria from 1% - 100%. The criteria weighting must total 100%.

An example of using criteria ratings would apply to your thought process when buying a new car. You mentally develop a list of key criteria: cost, quality, safety, and maintenance record. Each criteria is then assigned a weight depending on its importance. The Rating Matrix on the next page depicts what your decision might look like.

Solution Rating Matrix

Criteria		Weight	Solutions		
			Car "A"	Car "B"	Car "C"
Cost	10 = Low 1 = High	40%			
Quality	10 = High 1 = Low	30%			
Safety	10 = High 1 = Low	20%			
Maint. Costs	10 = Low 1 = High	10%			
Total Points		100%			
Notes					

Step 2 - Select the Best Solution

Once the C.I. Team has developed a list of key criteria and assigned a weight to each, the next step is to rate each of the solutions against each criteria (on a scale of 1 to 10). After rating each solution, multiply the rating by the weight percentage to arrive at the total score for that criteria. For example, Car "C" has a low sales price, therefore a Cost rating of 9. To arrive at the total points multiple 9 times 40% = Total score 3.6.

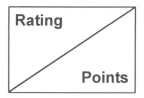

Points = Rating x Weight
3.6 = 9 x 40%

Criteria		Weight	Solutions		
			Car "A"	Car "B"	Car "C"
Cost	10 = Low 1 = High	40%	3 / 1.2	7 / 2.8	9 / 3.6
Quality	10 = High 1 = Low	30%	9 / 2.7	8 / 2.4	5 / 1.5
Safety	10 = High 1 = Low	20%	8 / 1.6	7 / 1.4	5 / 1.0
Maint. Costs	10 = Low 1 = High	10%	10 / 1.0	7 / .7	3 / .3
Total Points		100%	6.5	7.3	6.4
Notes			Expensive, nice features	Reasonable price, Good make/model	Inexpensive

Sum the total score for each criteria. The solutions with the highest score should be considered top priority for implementation. In the example, it is a toss-up between Car "A" and Car "C." Select the one that looks good.

Step 3 -Develop an Implementation Plan

After deciding on which solution to implement, a detailed plan should be developed. The plan should include (1) an Estimated Impact of Action Plan worksheet for all activities affected by the solution; and (2) Action Plan "To Do" list.

After selecting the best solution from the rating matrix, the C.I. Team's next step is to identify which Activities will be affected by the solution. An Activity can be affected in several ways:

> Total Cost (Increase or Decrease)
> Total Output Volume (Increase or Decrease)
> Cost per Output (Increase or Decrease)

A worksheet, like the one below, is a useful tool in calculating the total productivity improvement. Compare the results to your original goal. If the solution selected will not meet your goal, consider an alternative solution. See Appendix A for a completed example of both the following forms.

Estimated Impact of Action Plan

Department _____

Activities	Before			After			Net Change	
	Output Quantity	Cost per Output	Total Cost	Output Quantity	Cost per Output	Total Cost	Output Quantity	Total Cost
Variance								

While developing the Action Plan, keep in mind the following:

- Detailed action items for implementation
- Person responsible for implementing each action item
- Beginning and completion dates for each action item
- Estimated hours to complete each item
- Any costs incurred, including capital investments

To support this step, use a worksheet which provides the details for each action item. The worksheet will help ensure each step is carefully planned and coordinated. An example of a completed Action Plan is in Appendix A.

Action Plan "To Do" List					
Action Step Task/Activity	Responsible Person/Group	Begin Date	End Date	Estimated Hours	Costs
		Totals			

- Have you considered all departments, activities and processes that will be affected?
- Have you gotten necessary approvals from management?
- Have you considered all the resources required for implementation?

Step 4 - Implement

Once the plan is in place, you may want to prove or test the solution before full scale implementation. This may involve testing the plan in a small area before full rollout of the plan. Upon completion of the test area, the changes should be documented and distributed so that they can be incorporated into the full scale implementation action plan.

For example, one organization determined that an Activity Based Budget (ABB) was the solution to innovating the planning process. Instead of implementing ABB corporate wide, they targeted the Information and Systems (Computer) Departments to test ABB principals, procedures and benefits. This group was chosen for a logical reason: this group would be instrumental in designing a mainframe budget software to support a full scale implementation of ABB, so why not have the programmers be the test area for the proposed solution. It worked great, so the I.S. group proved that ABB is beneficial and learned how to program ABB by doing ABB.

Team Exercise

All too many projects and initiatives reach Step 4: *Implement* and then fail. Failure is typically caused by deferring implementation of the recommended changes, not as a result of a poor definition of the root causes or incorrect selection of a solution.

List the potential reasons why the solution you and your C.I. Team have chosen may never get implemented. Discuss ways to address each reason.

_____

_____

_____

_____

_____

Chapter Summary

Developing a C.I. Plan requires a disciplined approach to support Continuous Improvement.

There are four steps to developing a C.I. Plan:

1. Identify the key criteria - Develop a list of criteria that have direct influence over the desired outcome, such as: the impact on the customer, financial and time constraints, etc.

2. Select the best solution -One method for finding the solution that will have the most impact on the outcome would be a decision matrix.

3. Develop an Implementation Plan - After deciding which solution is best, implement it! Use a planning worksheet to provide detail for the action items, and a Gantt chart to graphically display the project in lengths of time.

4. Implement - Once the plan is in place, proof the plan and then implement it.

Notes

Step 5: Monitor the Improvement

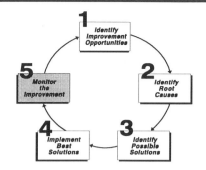

Meeting Notes

Attendees:
C.I. Team members

Objective:
Develop new Performance Measures and/or develop an Activity Based Budget

Meeting Time:
Ongoing 1 to 2 hours per session

Supplies:
Posterboard Marking Pens

Meeting Agenda

- Agree to meeting agenda and meeting length.

- Agree to the activities and/or process to be measured.

- Review Performance Measurement chapter and the examples in Appendices A, B & C.

- Develop Activity and Business Process Performance Measures for monitoring improvement plan.

- Define "To Do's".

- Set date for meeting with C.I. Committee or Senior Management to update them on the actual performance and results of the plan.

- Select another continuous improvement target and return to Step 1 of the unending process of improvement.

- Develop an Activity Based Budget for your department. See page 149 for the steps and format. Compare actual Activity costs on a quarterly basis to the Activity budget to measure your Continuous Improvement performance.

Performance Measurement

Whatever happened to Lou, the plant controller in Eli Goldratt's popular book, THE GOAL[1]? Lou and the accounting system did not play a proactive role in the book. Lou was mentioned at the beginning but not at the end. Why?

If you have read THE GOAL, you probably remember the saga of plant manager, Alex Rogo. Alex is told by his boss, Bill Peach, that the factory is going to be closed unless it turns a profit within the next three months. Peach says, "The future of our business depends upon our ability to increase productivity." Alex replies, "Everyone in the factory is working as hard as possible. How can the plant be more productive?"

Alex is confused and frustrated. The Profit & Loss statement shows a loss, but all the other financial performance measures look great. The cost per unit of their product is declining. The monthly cost accounting report issued by the plant controller, Lou, is covered with favorable variances to standard cost and budget.

Alex's friend, Jonah, interrupts and asks whether inventories are increasing. Alex answers "Yes". Jonah asks if customer complaints for missed delivery dates are increasing. Alex again answers yes.

"Alex," Jonah says, "It is clear to me that you're not running as efficient a plant as you think you are."

"The measurements say the opposite," Alex counters. "Are you trying to tell me my people are lying to me or something?"

"No," Jonah responds. "It is unlikely your people are lying to you. But your measurements definitely are."

Performance Measurement is the critical final step in the Continuous Improvement process. Measurement assures action and conformance to plan.

An old performance measurement saying states "You get what you measure." Another way of saying it is "Be careful what you ask for, because you might get it."

[1] THE GOAL, published by North River Press, Inc.

What you take for granted you cannot improve!

Performance Measurement

Many of your existing measures prevent Continuous Improvement. If a company's performance measure is to compared monthly sales to forecast, employees will respond to the performance measure to get an "attaboy" and "attagirl". Because the measurement is monthly, not daily, salesmen will procrastinate getting orders. Manufacturing will expedite the orders. Shipping will expedite the orders. The monthly performance measure focuses employees on shipping a forecasted volume of orders on the last day of the month.

Often organizations get into a repetitive monthly rut as a direct result of the end-of-month performance measure. They put off to the end of the month what they could do today. All too often 50% of the orders are received, produced and shipped the last week of the month. Is this practical? Obviously not. Employees are likely waiting for work in the first two weeks of the month and overworked the last two weeks.

While sales are important to any organization, we should not confuse Actual versus Forecasted Sales and many other existing performance measures as yardsticks for Continuous Improvement. In fact, many measures encourage employees to do just the opposite of improve.

> **Can you list 2-3 performance measures that encourage behavior inconsistent with the principles of continuous improvement?** Example: Indirect vs. Direct Headcount.
>
> 1. _____
>   _____
> 2. _____
>   _____
> 3. _____
>   _____

Three Principles of Performance Measurement

Effectively achieving and sustaining Continuous Improvement requires simple, relevant performance measures focused on activity output. Before we describe and recommend activity and process measures for your consideration and use, lets discuss three basic guiding principles of ABM performance measurement.

Principle 1 - Make Measures Simple

The best Continuous Improvement performance measures are:

- Easy to understand... by everyone.
- Easy to collect... accessible today.
- Timely... hourly, daily or weekly.
- Visible... posted on the wall
- Informative... no interpretation required

Principle 2 - Make Measures Relevant

The best Continuous Improvement performance measures are:

- Linked to company strategy... encourage actions that will result in achieving strategy
- Linked to the customer and their expectations
- Supportive of Continuous Improvement
- Under the control of those being measured

Principle 3 - Measure Output

The best Continuous Improvement performance measures are:

- Measures of <u>activity output</u> quantity, cost, time, and quality
- Measures of business <u>process output</u> quantity, cost, time, and quality
- Effective and efficient process controls
- Good predictors of the future
- Measures of output... not measures that simply encourage people and machines to look busy

Three Principles of Performance Measurement:

1) Keep them simple

2) Make them relevant

3) Focus on output

Activity & Process Performance Measures

In the Beginning is the End. In other words, to define a numerical activity performance measure to monitor a Continuous Improvement action plan, we must first consider the end goal or objective. Is the end goal a benchmarked best practice? Is the eventual goal perfection (i.e. zero defects)? Or is the goal an incremental change (i.e. 10% productivity improvement from last year's actual results)? Improvement is the direction... the goal is the destination.

As we have discussed in this handbook, some Continuous Improvement Process (CIP) solutions focus on an individual activity. Other solutions focus on series of interrelated activities or business processes. Performance measures to monitor the improvements, therefore, fall into two categories: (1) Activity Performance Measures and (2) Process Performance Measures. No matter what measures you select, remember to consider the three principles... simple, relevant and output focused.

Improvement is your direction... the goal of excellence is your destination.

Activity Performance Measures

Your action plans will focus on improving the cost, cycle time or quality of an activity. An action plan to reduce activity cost could increase or decrease activity cycle time or output quality. Conversely, an improvement idea that reduces activity cycle time could also reduce cost per output of an activity.

We recommend that you choose one or more of the activity based measures from the following pages. Select the one that best supports the intent and objectives of your action plan. You may want to report some performance measures frequently. For example, an output chart on a daily basis provides everyone in a department a simple method to measure workload and plan the impact of an action program. Other performance measures, such as a cost per output, should be done on a quarterly basis. Choose the measure and frequency that best meets your specific needs and resources.

A.   Value Added Activity Performance Measures

    1.   Output Quantity Trend Chart

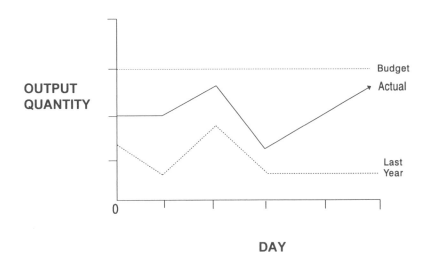

Measure activity output quantity by day, week or month. For example, measuring number of receipts per day or week provides a mirrored reflection of workload trend.

    2.   Output SPC Chart

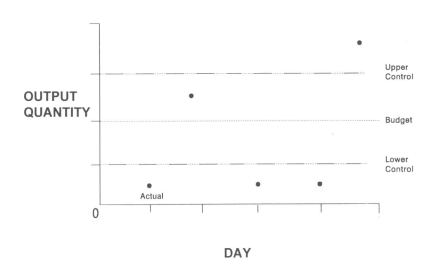

Use a Statistical Process Control (SPC) performance measure to monitor the quantity of output compared to predetermined standards. If your organization has SPC, this chart is a terrific way to link ABM and TQM.

Performance Measurement

Use a cost per output trend chart, normally on a quarterly basis, to measure productivity improvement of cost per activity outputs in your department.

3.   Cost Per Output Trend Chart

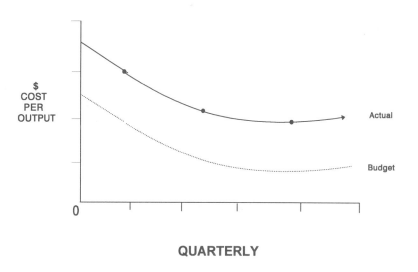

Cost per output can be applied to an SPC Chart to predict and measure nonconformance to your CIP action plan or budget.

4.   Cost per output SPC Chart

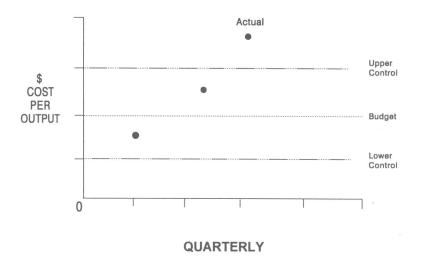

5.   Quality of Output Trend Chart

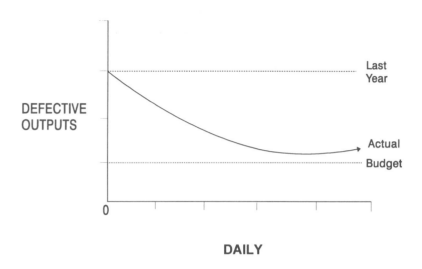

Ask the customer of your activity for a practical measure of quality. Measure the quality daily, weekly or monthly. For example, Purchasing could ask the Accounts Payable department the quality (accuracy) of purchase orders.

6.   Quality of Output SPC Chart

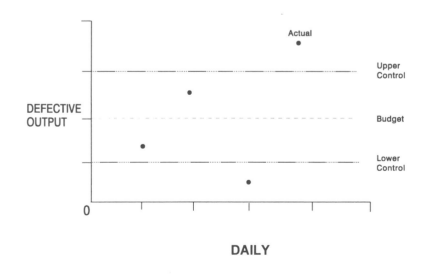

The Quality of Output could be utilized in an SPC Chart to monitor a process. For example, if the number of output defects fall outside predefined upper or lower limits, the activity is deemed out of control and immediate action is required.

The time it takes to produce an output can be measured. If your CIP action plan focuses on time reduction, this performance measure chart would be beneficial.

7.   Cycle Time of Output Trend Chart

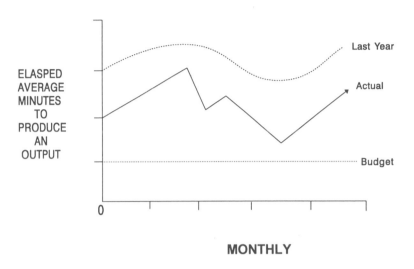

Sample periodically the elapsed time to produce an output in your department. Note the sample on an SPC Chart. For example, how long does it take to process a requisition in Purchasing? The elapsed time of a purchase order may be important to your CIP efforts.

8.   Cycle Time of Output SPC Chart

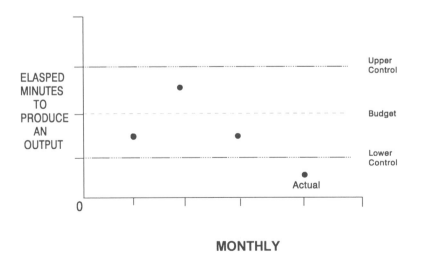

9. On Time Delivery of Output Trend Chart

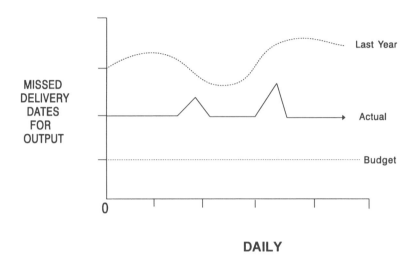

Did you produce the output when required by your internal or external customer? Here is a simple measurement chart to track performance to customer requested date and time.

10. Root Cause Quantity Trend Chart

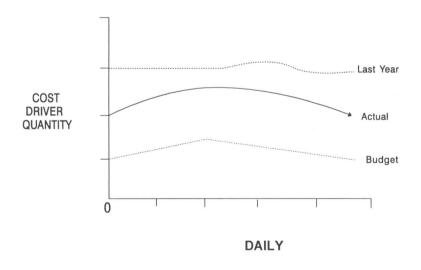

The root cause of an activity is typically the focus of your continuous improvement effort. Measure the quantity of the root cause on a daily, weekly or monthly basis.

Performance Measurement

11. Gross Cost of Departmental Activities...
an Activity Based Budget

Update the gross cost of every department's value and non-value activities at least once every three months using the Activity Based Budgeting worksheet (i.e., retrace actual spending to departmental activities and collect actual output quantities). Evaluate the gross cost of business processes at the same time.

BEFORE ACTION PLAN		Receive Material	Move Material	Expedite Material	Manage Employee	Do Admin. Task
COST	TOTAL	Primary/Value	Primary/Non-Value	Primary/Non-Value	Secondary/Value	Secondary/Value
Supplies	$88,000	$35,200	$15,000	$21,000	$6,240	$10,560
Depreciation	$186,000	$35,000	$110,000	$35,000	$3,000	$3,000
Salaries	$545,000	$179,850	$141,700	$81,750	$109,000	$32,700
Space	$51,000	$17,000	$17,000	$8,500	$5,100	$3,400
All Other	$74,000	$24,420	$19,240	$11,100	$14,800	$4,440
Total Cost	$944,000	$291,470	$302,940	$157,350	$138,140	$54,100
Output Measure Quantity		2,500	11,000	1,250	10	10
Output Measure		Receipts	Moves	Expedites	Employees	Employees
Cost per Output		$117	$28	$126	$13,814	$5,410

AFTER ACTION PLAN		Receive Material	Move Material	Expedite Material	Manage Employee	Do Admin. Task
COST	TOTAL	Primary/Value	Primary/Non-Value	Primary/Non-Value	Secondary/Value	Secondary/Value
Supplies	$75,000	$35,200	$15,000	$8,000	$6,240	$10,560
Depreciation	$161,800	$35,000	$110,000	$10,800	$3,000	$3,000
Salaries	$495,950	$179,850	$141,700	$32,700	$109,000	$32,700
Space	$51,000	$17,000	$17,000	$8,500	$5,100	$3,400
All Other	$65,900	$24,420	$19,240	$3,000	$14,800	$4,440
Total Cost	$849,650	$291,470	$302,940	$63,000	$138,140	$54,100
Output Measure Quantity		2,500	11,000	500	10	10
Output Measure		Receipts	Moves	Expedites	Employees	Employees
Cost per Output		$117	$28	$126	$13,814	$5,410

B.   Non-Value Added Activity Performance Measures

There are fewer performance measures recommended for non-value added activities than value for one simple reason. Your objective is to eliminate non-value activities... not improve their cost, time or quality. As a result, the list of measures to monitor an action plan related to a non-value added activity should be limited to the following three measures:

1.   Output Quantity Trend Chart

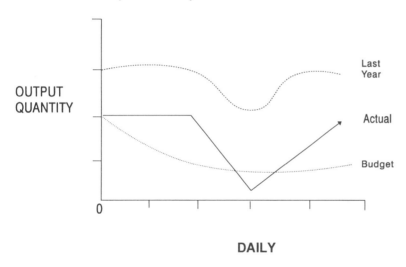

DAILY

2.   Cost Driver Quantity Trend Chart

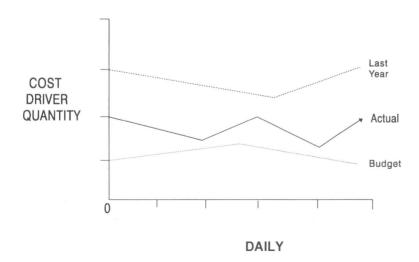

DAILY

3.   Gross cost of departmental activities quarterly

COST	TOTAL	Receive Material Primary/Value	Move Material Primary/Non-Value	Expedite Material Primary/Non-Value	Manage Employee Secondary/Value	Do Admin. Task Secondary/Value
Supplies	**$88,000**	$35,200	$15,000	$21,000	$6,240	$10,560
Depreciation	**$186,000**	$35,000	$110,000	$35,000	$3,000	$3,000
Salaries	**$545,000**	$179,850	$141,700	$81,750	$109,000	$32,700
Space	**$51,000**	$17,000	$17,000	$8,500	$5,100	$3,400
All Other	**$74,000**	$24,420	$19,240	$11,100	$14,800	$4,440
Total Cost	**$944,000**	**$291,470**	**$302,940**	**$157,350**	**$138,140**	**$54,100**
Output Measure Quantity		2,500	11,000	1,250	10	10
Output Measure		Receipts	Moves	Expedites	Employees	Employees
Cost per Output		$117	$28	$126	$13,814	$5,410

Business Process Performance Measures

Measure process output quantity by day, week or month. For example, measure the number of sales orders that come out of the last activity of the Sales Order Process.

The performance measures for a business process CIP action plan will be similar to those of a value added activity:

1. Output Quantity Trend Chart

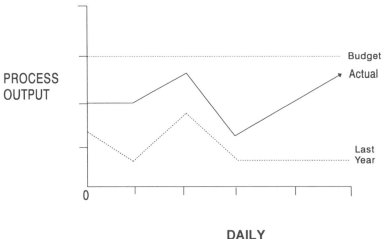

2. Output SPC Chart

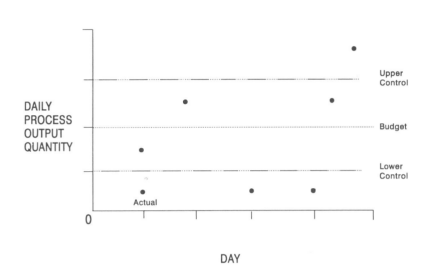

Use a Statistical Process Control (SPC) performance measure to monitor the quantity of output compared to predetermined standards. If your organization has SPC, this chart is a terrific way to link ABM and TQM.

3. Cost per Output Trend Chart

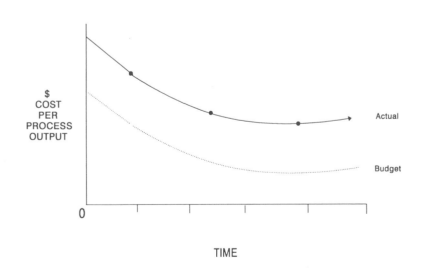

Use a cost per output trend chart, normally on a quarterly basis, to measure productivity improvement of cost per activity outputs in the process.

Performance Measurement

The cost per output can be applied to an SPC Chart to predict and measure nonconformance to your CIP action plan or budget.

4.   Cost per Output SPC Chart

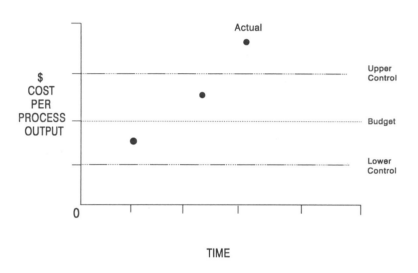

Ask the customer of your activity for a practical measure of process. Measure the quality daily, weekly or monthly. For example, the Procurement Process team should ask the Manufacturing Process team if the quality of parts meets their needs.

5.   Quality of Output Trend Chart

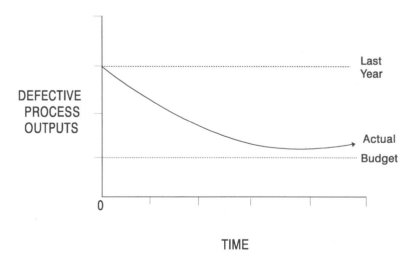

6. Quality of Output SPC Chart

The Quality of Output could be utilized in an SPC Chart to monitor a process. For example, if the number of output defects fall outside predefined upper or lower limits, the activity is deemed out of control and immediate action is required.

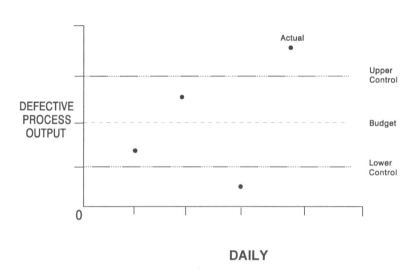

DAILY

7. Cycle Time of Process Trend (Pink Paper) Chart

The time it takes to produce an output can be measured. If your CIP action plan focuses on time reduction, this performance measure chart would be beneficial. Use a pink piece of paper stapled to the forms that flow through a process to measure cycle time. Have people in each process activity log the time they received the pink paper.

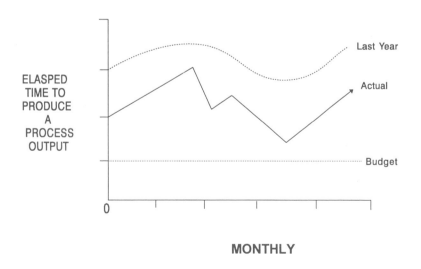

MONTHLY

Performance Measurement

Sample periodically the elapsed time to produce an output in your department. Note the sample on an SPC Chart. For example, how long does it take to process a requisition? The elapsed time of a purchase order may be important to your CIP efforts.

8. Cycle Time of Process SPC Chart

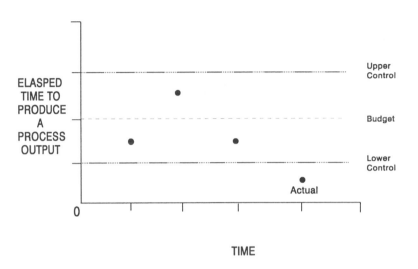

Did you produce the output when required by your internal or external customer? Here is a simple measurement chart to track performance to customer requested date and time.

9. On-Time Delivery of Output Chart

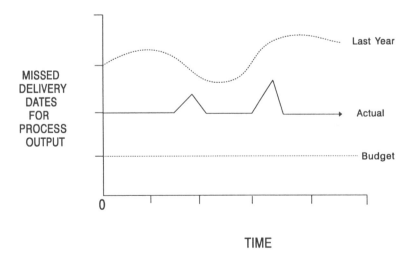

10.   Root Cause Quantity Trend Chart

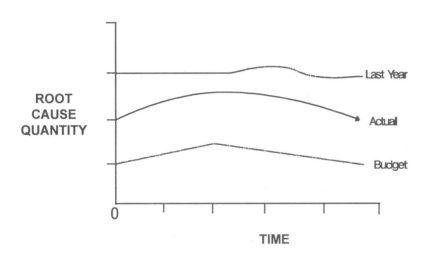

Update the gross cost of every department's Value and Non-Value Activities at least once every three months using the Activity Based Budgeting worksheet (i.e., retrace actual spending to departmental Activities and collect actual output quantities). Evaluate the gross cost of Business Processes at the same time.

11.   Gross Cost of Business Process Chart

ACTIVITIES	TOTAL COST	VALUE	NON-VALUE	DEPARTMENT	OUTPUT QTY.	COST PER OUTPUT
Run MRP	$700,000	$700,000	$0	Planning	100	$7,000
Issue Requisition	$145,000	$145,000	$0	Planning	2,200	$66
Issue Purchase Order	$250,000	$250,000	$0	Purchasing	1,800	$139
Handle Vendor Problem	$140,000	$0	$140,000	Purchasing	450	$311
Expedite Purchase Order	$145,000	$0	$145,000	Purchasing	440	$330
Certify Vendors	$175,000	$175,000	$0	Purchasing	12	$14,583
Receive Material	$291,470	$291,470	$0	Receiving	2,500	$117
Move Material	$302,940	$0	$302,940	Receiving	11,000	$28
Expedite Material	$157,350	$0	$157,350	Receiving	1,250	$126
Inspect Material	$225,000	$0	$225,000	Quality	2,500	$90
Expedite Material	$80,000	$0	$80,000	Quality	500	$160
Reject Material	$90,000	$0	$90,000	Quality	400	$225
Certify Vendor	$185,000	$185,000	$0	Quality	15	$12,333
Return Goods to Vendor	$60,000	$0	$60,000	Quality	375	$160
Pay Vendor Invoice	$205,000	$205,000	$0	Accounting	1,500	$137
Contact Vendor	$72,000	$0	$72,000	Accounting	250	$288
Issue Debit Memo	$65,000	$0	$65,000	Accounting	375	$173
Store Material	$102,000	$0	$102,000	Warehouse	1,800	$57
Cycle Count Inventory	$40,150	$0	$40,150	Warehouse	2,500	$16
TOTAL COST	**$3,430,910**	**$1,951,470**	**$1,479,440**			
TOTAL PERCENT	**100%**	**57%**	**43%**			

Chapter Summary

SPECIAL NOTE:

The best performance measure is the one we do not need. You may have to reread this statement a few times for it to sink in. We want you to keep two important things in mind as you define your measures and monitor your performance:

(1) Do not automatically think that adding more performance measures makes your organization more in control or more efficient. When you add a measure, look at eliminating others, especially those that encourage behavior opposite of continuous improvement.

(2) Continuous improvement is a direction. Perfection is the destination. Define your solutions and action plans for each activity and process with this... Continually ask yourself "How can I design this process where we cannot make a mistake?" People don't make mistakes. Processes allow people (and machines) to make a mistake. When a best practice, mistake-proof process is defined and established, you will not need a performance measure for that process.

The best performance measure is the one we do not need. As you define your performance measures and monitor your performance, remember: 1) Do not think that adding more performance measures makes your organization more in control or more efficient; and 2) Continuous Improvement and Perfection are directions. Define your solutions and action plans for each activity and process with this... There are three principles of Performance Measurement:
1) Keep it simple
2) Make it relevant
3) Focus on output

Performance measures fall into two categories:

Activity Performance Measures:
    A.   Value Added Activity Performance Measures
        1.   Output Quantity Trend
        2.   Output SPC Chart
        3.   Cost per Output Trend
        4.   Cost per Output SPC Chart
        5.   Quality of Output Trend
        6.   Quality of Output SPC Chart
        7.   Cycle Time of Output Trend
        8.   Cycle Time of Output SPC Chart
        9.   On Time Delivery of Output Trend
        10.   Cost Driver (Root Cause) Quantity Trend
        11.   Gross Cost of Departmental Activities
    B.   Non-Value Added Activity Performance Measures
        1.   Output Quantity Trend
        2.   Cost Driver Quantity Trend
        3.   Gross Cost of Departmental Activities

Process Performance Measures
        1.   Output Quantity Trend
        2.   Output SPC Chart
        3.   Cost per Output Trend
        4.   Cost per Output SPC Chart
        5.   Quality of Output Trend
        6.   Quality of Output SPC Chart
        7.   Cycle Time of Process Trend (pink paper)
        8.   Cycle Time of Process SPC Chart
        9.   On Time Delivery of Output
        10.   Cost Driver (Root Cause) Quantity Trend
        11.   Gross Cost of Business Process

 **Notes**

Activity Based Budgeting

For many organizations, the budget represents a senior management "wish list". A carrot to dangle in front of the organization in hopes that improved results might happen or could happen. You sit impatiently every month waiting to be happy or sad. The anticipation following the end of each month can be excruciating for a manager. If your variance to budget is favorable this month, you can be happy for another 30 days. If the variance is unfavorable, you are immediately unhappy, and so is your boss.

This annual ritual of posturing, politics, and frustration typically consumes 3 to 6 months of an organization's time. The resulting budget document is used on a monthly basis as the yardstick of organizational success or failure. The president of the company, after impatiently awaiting receipt of the monthly actual versus budget report is also left alone to be happy or sad, but never smarter. He knows what happened but not why!

Activity Based Budgeting

Using Activities to budget and measure performance has been basically overlooked by most implementors of Activity-based cost systems.

Activity Based Budgeting is a process of planning and controlling the expected activities of an organization. Activity Based Budgeting links work activities with the strategic cost, time and quality objectives of the organization. An Activity Based Budget focuses on activities. Budgeted costs are determined after the activity workload is defined. In other words, focus on the work, secondarily the worker.

"The president of the company, after impatiently awaiting receipt of the monthly actual versus budget report, is also left alone to be happy or sad, but never smarter. He knows what happened, but not why!"

Top 10 Weaknesses of Traditional Budgeting

⑩
Does not identify or quantify waste.

⑨
Does not identify work or workloads

⑧
Focuses on cuts, not continuous improvement.

⑦
Focuses on functions, not processes.

⑥
Does not identify root causes of costs.

⑤
Does not identify levels of service.

④
Does not link to the strategic plan.

③
Focuses on input (costs) not output.

②
Focuses on costs, not quality or time.

①
Does not provide a common language that supports common sense.

Activity Based Budgeting

Steps To Activity Based Budgeting

1. Define activities for budget period

2. Define activity workloads for budget period

3. Establish each activity's cost per output

4. Determine budget resource requirements

5. Compare budget to actual resources and plan necessary changes

An Activity Based Budget can be effectively and efficiently completed in 30 days.

Five Steps to Activity Based Budgeting

Step 1 - Define Activities for Budget Period

The first step is to determine what activities the department (activity center) plan to perform next year for the budget time period. Typically, the activities will be the same or similar to the current period. What will differ in the budget period will be the volume of activity output, often referred to as the activity workload and the costs consumed by the Activities. The department manager should create or re-interview for accuracy the current departmental activities, output (workload) and costs.

Step 2 - Define Activity Workloads for Budget Period

Define estimated budget period activity output quantities by combining product related workloads , non-product related activities and project related activities. To determine activity output measure volumes for activities traceable to a product or service, the product sales demand is multiplied times the product Bill of Activity. If you do not have an ABC cost system, you can still estimate product related activity workloads. Simply determine the percentage increase in production volume for the budget period and multiply times current activity output quantities. For example, if production will increase 10% next year, we can assume 10% more output for each production process activity. The example on the next page depicts an Activity Based Budget worksheet for a Receiving Department. Next year company plans are to produce a product volume of 1,700. For each product produced, two receipts of material must be performed. The manager of the Receiving department can, therefore, budget the number of receipts required for next year to be 3,400 (two receipts times 1,700). Number of moves are estimated to increase to 13,500, but expedites drop to 600 due to 1993 Continuous Improvement action plans. The number of employees, ten, is estimated to stay the same.

Receiving Department

ACTUAL '93	TOTAL	VALUE	NON-VALUE	NON-VALUE	VALUE	VALUE
Activities		Receive Material	Move Material	Expedite Material	Manage Employee	Do Admin Tasks
Supplies	$88,000	$35,200	$15,000	$21,000	$6,240	$10,560
Depreciation	$186,000	35,000	110,000	35,000	3,000	3,000
Salaries	$545,000	179,850	141,700	81,750	109,000	32,700
Space	$51,000	17,000	17,000	8,500	5,100	3,400
All Other	$74,000	24,420	19,240	11,100	14,800	4,440
TOTAL	$944,000	$291,470	$302,940	$157,350	$138,140	$54,100
Activity Output Measure		# of Receipts	# of Moves	# of Expedites	# of Employees	# of Employees
1993 Output Volume		2,500	11,000	1,250	10	10
1993 $/Output		$117	$28	$126	$13,814	$5,410
TOTAL	$944,000	$291,470	$302,940	$157,350	$138,140	$54,100
BUDGET '94	**TOTAL**					
Activities		Receive Material	Move Material	Expedite Material	Manage Employee	Do Admin Tasks
1994 Output Volume		3,400	13,500	600	10	10
Budget $/Output						
Total Budget (A)						
Supplies						
Depreciation						
Salaries						
Space						
All Other						
TOTAL (B)						
VARIANCE (A-B)						

Step 1 — (annotation pointing to Supplies row of ACTUAL '93)

Step 2 — (annotation pointing to 1994 Output Volume row)

Step 3 - Establish Each Activity's Cost Per Output

Define the budget cost per output for each activity. For example, the Receiving Department manager might initially assume the budgeted cost per activity for next year must be at least 10% less than this year's actual to comply with a corporate productivity guideline. The manager would, therefore, reduce the cost per receipt from $117.00 to $105.30 per receipt. This means that the manager and C.I. Team must find a way to offset the inflation of activity resources to meet the budgeted cost per output.

Two of the department's activities though are non-value added. In principal, it would be better for the organization if the department could reduce the budgeted output volumes of non-value activities. Instead of reducing the cost per expedite, the focus should be on reducing the quantity of expedites. The manager preparing the budget should utilize his/her C.I. Team to use the Five Step Continuous Improvement Process to improve the productivity of the department for the upcoming budget period.

A budget should be based on knowledge of how good the organization can and should be. The budget should constitute an achievable goal. Developing an achievable budget is often difficult because most managers develop a budget based on what they should spend, not on what they do (activities), that consumes the budgeted costs.

Activity Based Budgeting

The Receiving Department manager might prepare the Receiving Department budget by using the following assumptions:

A)   Reduce the cost per receipt from $117.00 to $100.00 based on a benchmarking study with a sister plant.

B)   Because no Action Plan has been defined to reduce the number of moves, the manager elects to reduce the cost per move by 10% ($28 to $25).

C)   The cost per expedite should not increase above the $126 experienced in 1993.

D)   The cost per output of the two secondary activities (Manage Employee and Do Admin. Tasks) in 1993 are 20% higher than other similar departments.   A 20% reduction is therefore budgeted.

Receiving Department

ACTUAL '93	TOTAL	VALUE	NON-VALUE	NON-VALUE	VALUE	VALUE
Activities		Receive Material	Move Material	Expedite Material	Manage Employee	Do Admin Tasks
Supplies	$88,000	$35,200	$15,000	$21,000	$6,240	$10,560
Depreciation	$186,000	35,000	110,000	35,000	3,000	3,000
Salaries	$545,000	179,850	141,700	81,750	109,000	32,700
Space	$51,000	17,000	17,000	8,500	5,100	3,400
All Other	$74,000	24,420	19,240	11,100	14,800	4,440
TOTAL	$944,000	$291,470	$302,940	$157,350	$138,140	$54,100
Activity Output Measure		# of Receipts	# of Moves	# of Expedites	# of Employees	# of Employees
1993 Output Volume		2,500	11,000	1,250	10	10
1993 $/Output		$117	$28	$126	$13,814	$5,410
TOTAL	$944,000	$291,470	$302,940	$157,350	$138,140	$54,100
BUDGET '94	TOTAL					
Activities		Receive Material	Move Material	Expedite Material	Manage Employee	Do Admin Tasks
1994 Output Volume		3,400	13,500	600	10	10
Budget $/Output	Step 3	$100	$25	$126	$11,051	$4,328
Total Budget (A)						
Supplies						
Depreciation						
Salaries						
Space						
All Other						
TOTAL (B)						
VARIANCE (A-B)						

Step 4 - Determine Budget Resource Requirements

Determine budgeted resource requirements by multiplying 1994 activity output volume by cost per output. By multiplying the volume of receipts budgeted for next year, 3,400 times the budgeted cost per output of $100.00, the result would be $340,000 in resources required next year to perform this activity. Performing this calculation for all five Receiving Department activities would result in a total budgeted resource requirement of $906,890.

Top 10 Strengths of Activity Based Budgeting, cont.

Activity Based Budgets identify levels of service between departments.

Activity Based Budgets begin by focusing on the strategic objectives of the company and then identifying the activities needed to meet those objectives.

Activity Based Budgets focus on required vs. discretionary activity outputs.

Activity Based Budgets focus on activity, cost, time and quality.

Activity Based Budgets use a common language of activities.

Receiving Department

ACTUAL '93	TOTAL	VALUE	NON-VALUE	NON-VALUE	VALUE	VALUE
Activities		Receive Material	Move Material	Expedite Material	Manage Employee	Do Admin Tasks
Supplies	$88,000	$35,200	$15,000	$21,000	$6,240	$10,560
Depreciation	$186,000	35,000	110,000	35,000	3,000	3,000
Salaries	$545,000	179,850	141,700	81,750	109,000	32,700
Space	$51,000	17,000	17,000	8,500	5,100	3,400
All Other	$74,000	24,420	19,240	11,100	14,800	4,440
TOTAL	$944,000	$291,470	$302,940	$157,350	$138,140	$54,100
Activity Output Measure		# of Receipts	# of Moves	# of Expedites	# of Employees	# of Employees
1993 Output Volume		2,500	11,000	1,250	10	10
1993 $/Output		$117	$28	$126	$13,814	$5,410
TOTAL	$944,000	$291,470	$302,940	$157,350	$138,140	$54,100
BUDGET '94	**TOTAL**					
Activities		Receive Material	Move Material	Expedite Material	Manage Employee	Do Admin Tasks
1994 Output Volume		3,400	13,500	600	10	10
Budget $/Output		$100	$25	$126	$11,051	$4,328
Total Budget (A)	$906,890	$340,000	$337,500	$75,600	$110,510	$43,280
Supplies						
Depreciation						
Salaries						
Space						
All Other						
TOTAL (B)						
VARIANCE (A-B)						

(Step 4 circled next to Total Budget (A) row)

Step 5 - Compare Budgeted to Actual Resources

Develop a budget by resource cost that matches the activity budget of $906,890 and submit to management for approval. The Receiving Department's budget of $906,890 can be achieved next year by:

- Reduce spending for expedite forms and office supplies

- Four people are no longer needed for expediting. Two people were redeployed to the Receive Material activity, one person to Move Material and one person to the Manufacturing Department. One supervisor was also redeployed to Manufacturing.

Receiving Department

ACTUAL '93	TOTAL	VALUE	NON-VALUE	NON-VALUE	VALUE	VALUE
Activities		Receive Material	Move Material	Expedite Material	Manage Employee	Do Admin Tasks
Supplies	$88,000	$35,200	$15,000	$21,000	$6,240	$10,560
Depreciation	$186,000	35,000	110,000	35,000	3,000	3,000
Salaries	$545,000	179,850	141,700	81,750	109,000	32,700
Space	$51,000	17,000	17,000	8,500	5,100	3,400
All Other	$74,000	24,420	19,240	11,100	14,800	4,440
TOTAL	$944,000	$291,470	$302,940	$157,350	$138,140	$54,100
Activity Output Measure		# of Receipts	# of Moves	# of Expedites	# of Employees	# of Employees
1993 Output Volume		2,500	11,000	1,250	10	10
1993 $/Output		$117	$28	$126	$13,814	$5,410
TOTAL	$944,000	$291,470	$302,940	$157,350	$138,140	$54,100
BUDGET '94	TOTAL					
Activities		Receive Material	Move Material	Expedite Material	Manage Employee	Do Admin Tasks
1994 Output Volume		3,400	13,500	600	10	10
Budget $/Output		$100	$25	$126	$11,051	$4,328
Total Budget (A)	$906,890	$340,000	$337,500	$75,600	$110,510	$43,280
Supplies	$75,200	$38,000	$16,000	$13,000	$3,000	$5,200
Depreciation	$186,000	35,000	110,000	35,000	3,000	3,000
Salaries	$516,990	220,000	160,000	15,100	93,410	28,480
Space	$51,000	17,000	17,000	8,500	5,100	3,400
All Other	$77,700	30,000	34,500	4,000	6,000	3,200
TOTAL (B)	$906,890	340,000	337,500	75,600	110,510	43,280
VARIANCE (A-B)	$0	$0	$0	$0	$0	$0

Step 5

Team Exercise:

List your frustrations with your current budget process:

_____

_____

_____

_____

_____

_____

_____

_____

_____

_____

_____

_____

_____

How will ABM address each concern?

_____

_____

_____

_____

_____

_____

_____

_____

_____

Chapter Summary

Activity Based Budgeting is the process of planning and controlling the expected activities of an organization, linking the work (activity) of the organization with cost, time and quality objectives.

An Activity Based Budget can be effectively and efficiently completed in 30 days. To create an Activity Based Budget, follow these steps:

1. Define the activities for the budget period — The activities will typically be similar to the activities in this year's budget.

2. Define the activity workloads for the budget period — Combine product related workloads, non-product related activities and project related activities to define the budget period activity output quantities.

3. Establish each activity's cost per output based on productivity improvement targets.

4. Determine budget resource requirements - Multiply activity output volume by the cost per output.

5. Compare budget to actual resources - Develop a budget by matching resource costs to the activity plan.

 **Notes**

Activity Analysis and Activity Accounting Summary

Receiving Department

COST	TOTAL	Receive Material	Move Material	Expedite Material	Manage Employee	Do Admin. Task
		Primary/Value	Primary/Non-Value	Primary/Non-Value	Secondary/Value	Secondary/Value
Supplies	$88,000	$35,200	$15,000	$21,000	$6,240	$10,560
Depreciation	$186,000	$35,000	$110,000	$35,000	$3,000	$3,000
Salaries	$545,000	$179,850	$141,700	$81,750	$109,000	$32,700
Space	$51,000	$17,000	$17,000	$8,500	$5,100	$3,400
All Other	$74,000	$24,420	$19,240	$11,100	$14,800	$4,440
Total Cost	$944,000	$291,470	$302,940	$157,350	$138,140	$54,100
Output Measure Quantity		2,500	11,000	1,250	10	10
Output Measure		Receipts	Moves	Expedites	Employees	Employees
Cost per Output		$117	$28	$126	$13,814	$5,410

Scenario

The Receiving Department manager has just completed an ABM analysis of his department. Senior management has requested a productivity improvement of 10% by next year. The Receiving Department manager believes a majority of the department's opportunities for improvement are related to Non-Value Added Activities. The manager has developed an employee Receiving Department C.I. Team to execute the Five Step Continuous Improvement Process.

Step 1: Identify Improvement Opportunities

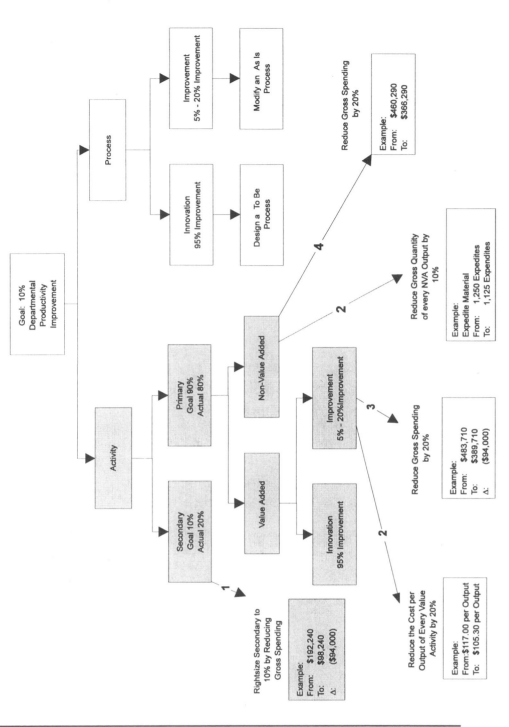

There are four options that should be considered to identify improvement opportunities. Improving productivity by 10% in this department requires a $94,000 change.

Option 1: Reduce spending on the two Secondary Activities;

Option 2: Reduce the Cost per Output of each Value Added Activity and simultaneously reduce the gross quantity of every Non-Value Activity;

Option 3: Reduce the gross spending of Value Activities by 20% or $94,000;

Option 4: Reduce the gross spending of Non-Value Activities by 20% or $94,000.

Continued with Step 1: Identify Improvement Opportunities

	ACTUAL	BENCHMARK
Value Added	51%	100%
Non-Value Added	49%	0%
Primary	80%	90%
Secondary	20%	10%

Tree diagram:

- Identify Improvement Opportunities
  - Activity
    - Secondary Goal 10%
    - Primary Goal 90%
    - Value Added
      - Innovation 95% Improvement
      - Improvement 5%-20% Improvement
    - Non-Value Added Goal 0%
  - Process
    - Innovation 95% Improvement
      - Design a "To Be" Process
    - Improvement 5%-20% Improvement
      - Modify an "As Is" Process

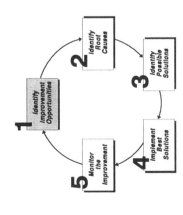

1. Identify Improvement Opportunities
2. Identify Root Causes
3. Identify Possible Solutions
4. Implement Best Solutions
5. Monitor the Improvement

Using the ABM Information generated for the Receiving Department, the Receiving Department C.I. Team analyzed their activity classifications... Value vs. Non-Value, and Primary vs. Secondary. The analysis revealed an extremely high Non-Value Added Percentage. The Receiving Department C.I. Team, therefore, decided the greatest opportunity for improvement was Option 4, reducing or eliminating Non-Value Added Activities. The Receiving Department C.I. Team selected the most expensive Non-Value Activity, "Expedite Material", to focus their Continuous Improvement effort.

Step 2: Identify Root Causes

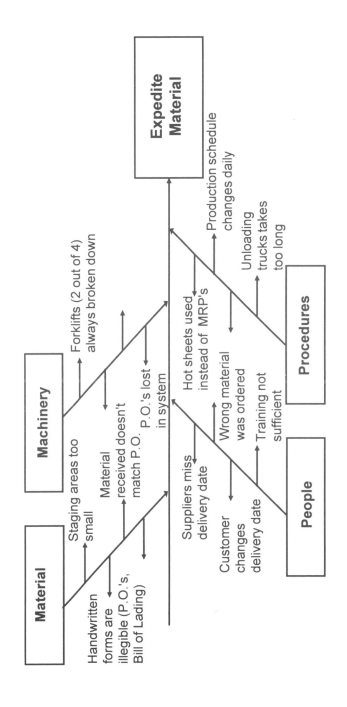

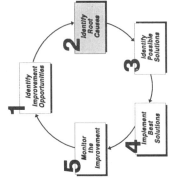

Using a Cause-and-Effect Diagram, the Receiving Department C.I. Team defined four main "root cause" categories for the activity "Expedite Material": People, Procedures, Material and Machinery. Once the four main cause categories were established, the Receiving Department C.I. Team listed several causes for the activity "Expedite Material" on each branch of the diagram.

Continued with Step 2: Identify Root Causes

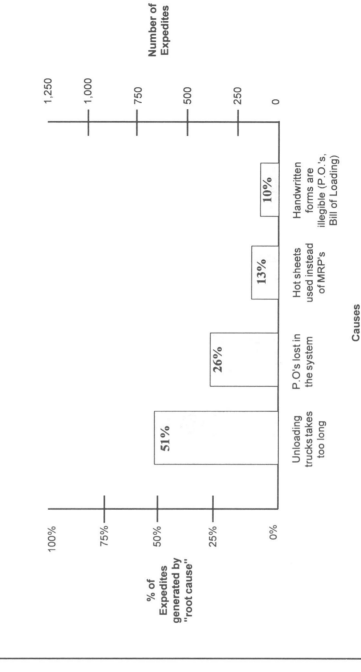

To narrow the list of causes generated during the Cause-and-Effect Diagramming session, the Receiving Department C.I. Team performed a Pareto Analysis. The C.I. Team estimated how many of the 1,250 outputs of the activity "Expedite Material" were associated with the four most likely root causes chosen for Pareto Analysis. The Pareto Analysis revealed "Unloading trucks taking too long" caused over 50% of the expedites to occur. The Receiving Department C.I. Team decided to focus on why unloading trucks takes so long.

Continued with Step 2: Identify Root Causes

Q: Why does unloading the truck take too long?

A: *There are not enough forklifts.*

→

Q: Why are there not enough forklifts.

A: *Two out of four forklifts broken.*

→

Q: Why are two out of four forklifts broken?

A: *Because they run out of oil and water.*

→

Q: Why do they run out of oil and water??

A: *Basic maintenance not performed.*

→

Q: Why is basic maintenance not performed?

A: *Daily start-up checks not performed.*

1 Identify Improvement Opportunities

2 Identify Root Causes

3 Identify Possible Solutions

4 Implement Best Solutions

5 Monitor the Improvement

The Receiving Department C.I. Team then decided to use the Five Why's approach to determine the root cause "Why unloading trucks takes too long". After asking "Why?" five times, the Receiving Department C.I. Team arrived at the root cause why unloading trucks taking too long: Daily start-up checks not being performed on the forklifts before use. The Receiving Department C.I. Team now proceeds to Step 3 to generate solutions for getting daily start-up checks performed.

Step 3: Identify Possible Solutions

Get daily start-up checks performed on the forklifts

Procedure Change	Policy Change	Equipment Change	Responsibility Change
Create startup checklist	Have vendor deliver materials directly to department	Purchase more forklifts	Maintenance performs checks
Make start-ups a part of employee reviews	Smaller delivery sizes so forklift not needed	Lease forklifts, they perform maintenance	Assign one employee responsible to come in early and do checks
Define first 15 min. of shifts for start-up checks		Install indicator lights on forklifts, signals failure	
Provide additional training			
Start-up checklist and sign-off sheet			

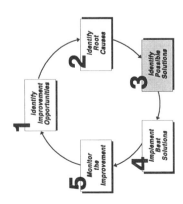

1 — Identify Improvement Opportunities
2 — Identify Root Causes
3 — Identify Possible Solutions
4 — Implement Best Solutions
5 — Monitor the Improvement

Having defined a root cause of Expediting, the Receiving Department C.I. Team proceeded to generate a list of possible solutions for getting "Daily start-up checks performed". The Receiving Department C.I. Team selected the Storyboarding technique as its Continuous Improvement tool. Numerous ideas were written on 3"x5" cards and put on the wall. The ideas were then grouped into four (4) types of changes: Procedure, Policy, Equipment, and Responsibility.

Step 4: Implement a C.I. Plan

Criteria	Weight	Solutions			
		Daily Start-up Checklist	Lease Forklift	Eliminate forklifts/ use small lot sizes	Install indicator lights
Cost of Solution (How much will it cost to implement the solution?) 10 = Low 1 = High	30%				
Effectiveness of Solution (How effective would the solution be in addressing root causes and solving the problem?) 10 = High 1 = Low	30%				
Probability of Success (How likely is it that the solution itself could successfully be implemented?) 10 = High 1 = Low	20%				
Resistance (How much resistance might there be to implementing the solution?) 10 = Low 1 = High	10%				
Ease of Implementation (How easy would it be to implement the solution?) 10 = High 1 = Low	10%				
Total	100%				

Rating / Points (rating x weight)

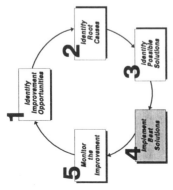

1 Identify Improvement Opportunities
2 Identify Root Causes
3 Identify Possible Solutions
4 Implement Best Solutions
5 Monitor the Improvement

After identifying a variety of solutions to "Getting the daily start-up checks performed", the Receiving Department C.I. Team proceeded to select the best solution to implement. The Receiving Department C.I. Team used a decision matrix to analyze their choices. The criteria to evaluate the possible solutions were: (1) cost, (2) effectiveness, (3) probability, (4) resistance, and (5) ease. The Receiving Department C.I. Team, working with their department manager, assigned a weight to each criteria. For example, cost was given a 30% impedance factor.

Continued with Step 4: Implement a C.I. Plan

Criteria	Weight	Solutions			
		Daily Start-up Checklist	Lease Forklift	Eliminate forklifts/ use small lot sizes	Install indicator lights
Cost of Solution 10 = Low / 1 = High (How much will it cost to implement the solution?)	30%	10 / 3.0	1 / .3	5 / 1.5	7 / 2.1
Effectiveness of Solution 10 = High / 1 = Low (How effective would the solution be in addressing root causes and solving the problem?)	30%	7 / 2.1	7 / 2.1	5 / 1.5	6 / 1.8
Probability of Success 10 = High / 1 = Low (How likely is it that the solution itself could successfully be implemented?)	20%	10 / 2.0	10 / 2.0	7 / 1.4	6 / 1.2
Resistance 10 = Low / 1 = High (How much resistance might there be to implementing the solution?)	10%	4 / .4	5 / .5	1 / .1	8 / .8
Ease of Implementation 10 = High / 1 = Low (How easy would it be to implement the solution?)	10%	10 / 1.0	3 / .3	4 / .4	7 / .7
Total	100%	8.5	5.2	4.9	6.6

Key: Rating / Points (rating × weight)

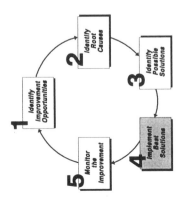

Each of the four proposed solutions were then rated from 1 to 10 for each of the five criteria. For example, creating a daily start-up checklist was rated a 10 because of its low cost to implement. The 10 rating was multiplied by the 30% weight factor, resulting in a total of 3.0 points. After each solution was rated, the points are totaled. Using the decision matrix, the Receiving Department C.I. Team decided the most effective and efficient solution was to develop and have each forklift driver perform a daily start-up check before using the equipment to insure oil and water levels are satisfactory. (Total score = 8.5)

Continued with Step 4: Implement a C.I. Plan

Estimated Impact of Action Plan

Receiving Department

	Before			After			Net Change	
	Output Quantity	Cost per Output	Total Cost	Output Quantity	Cost per Output	Total Cost	Output Quantity	Total Cost
Receive Material	No change							
Move Material	No change							
Expedite Material	1,250	$126	$157,350	500	$126	$63,000	-750	-$94,350
Manage Employee	No change							
Do Admin. Task	No change							
Totals								-$94,350

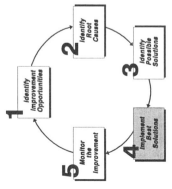

Before the Receiving Department C.I. Team developed their Action Plan, they estimated the impact of that Plan on all of their departmental activities. The team determines that the only Activity impacted by their checklist improvement plan was "Expedite Material". They estimated the impact to be a reduction of 750 expedites. If achieved, the estimated savings would be $94,350 (750 outputs x $126 per output). The next step to confirm reasonableness was to create a revised resource plan for reach Activity in the department.

Continued with Step 4: Implement a C.I. Plan

Action Plan

Action Step Task/Activity	Responsible Person/Group	Begin Date	End Date	Estimated Hours	Costs
Develop checklist	Receiving & Maintenance Department	7/1	7/5	2 hours	$150
Review checklist w/ supervisors	Forklift driver & Receiving Supervisor	7/8	7/8	1 hour	$50
Train forklift driver on checklist	Forklift drivers & Maintenance	7/10	7/10	1 hour	$75
Do weekly follow-up	Receiving Supervisor	7/10	9/30	3 hours	$150
Implement and evaluate for effectiveness	Receiving Supervisor & Employees	9/30	9/30	2 hours	$200
			Totals	9 hours	$625

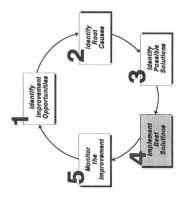

After selecting "Develop a daily checklist" as the improvement action to reduce expedites, the Receiving Department C.I. Team developed an Improvement Action Plan. Costs of $625 were considered minimal, and therefore, not added to any of the departmental Activities. The Action Plan and assigned responsibilities were very important if the plan was to be successfully implemented.

Step 5: Monitor the Improvement

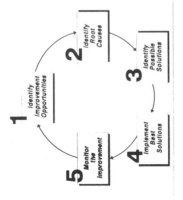

To develop a revised Activity Based Budget, the 500 remaining expedites are multiplied by the previous $126 cost per expedite (500 x $126 = $63,000). The Receiving Department C.I. Team develops an Expedite Material activity resource plan that matches the $63,000. Each cost is analyzed. They determine the following changes are reasonable and achievable:

	Before	After
- Reduce expedite forms	$21,000	$8,000
- Sell one forklift	$35,000	$10,800
- Transfer 2 employees to manufacturing	$81,750	$32,700
- Space (no change)	$8,500	$8,500
- Reduce phone calls (all other)	$11,100	$3,000
Total	$157,350	$63,000

BEFORE ACTION PLAN

COST	TOTAL	Receive Material Primary/Value	Move Material Primary/Non-Value	Expedite Material Primary/Non-Value	Manage Employee Secondary/Value	Do Admin. Task Secondary/Value
Supplies	$88,000	$35,200	$15,000	$21,000	$6,240	$10,560
Depreciation	$186,000	$35,000	$110,000	$35,000	$3,000	$3,000
Salaries	$545,000	$179,850	$141,700	$81,750	$109,000	$32,700
Space	$51,000	$17,000	$17,000	$8,500	$5,100	$3,400
All Other	$74,000	$24,420	$19,240	$11,100	$14,800	$4,440
Total Cost	$944,000	$291,470	$302,940	$157,350	$138,140	$54,100
Output Measure	Quantity	Receipts	Moves	Expedites	Employees	Employees
Output		2,500	11,000	1,250	10	10
Cost per Output		$117	$28	$126	$13,814	$5,410

AFTER ACTION PLAN

COST	TOTAL	Receive Material Primary/Value	Move Material Primary/Non-Value	Expedite Material Primary/Non-Value	Manage Employee Secondary/Value	Do Admin. Task Secondary/Value
Supplies	$75,000	$35,200	$15,000	$8,000	$6,240	$10,560
Depreciation	$161,800	$35,000	$110,000	$10,800	$3,000	$3,000
Salaries	$495,950	$179,850	$141,700	$32,700	$109,000	$32,700
Space	$51,000	$17,000	$17,000	$8,500	$5,100	$3,400
All Other	$65,900	$24,420	$19,240	$3,000	$14,800	$4,440
Total Cost	$849,650	$291,470	$302,940	$63,000	$138,140	$54,100
Output Measure	Quantity	Receipts	Moves	Expedites	Employees	Employees
Output		2,500	11,000	500	10	10
Cost per Output		$117	$28	$126	$13,814	$5,410

Continued with Step 5: Monitor the Improvement

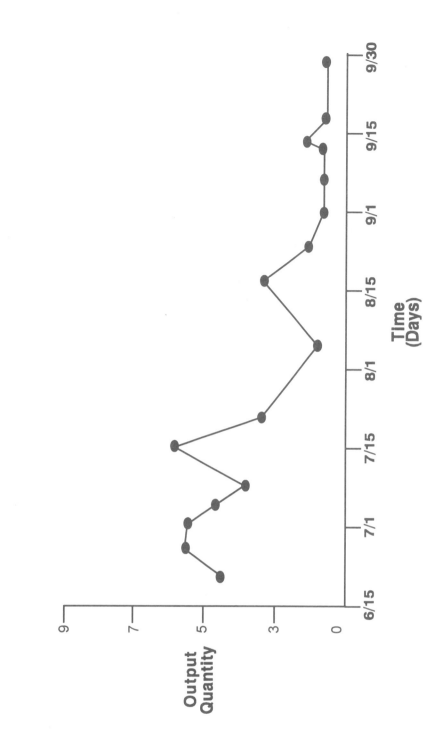

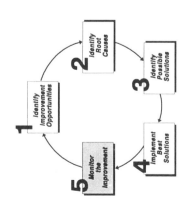

To measure their improvement efforts on a daily basis, the Receiving Department C.I. Team developed a simple performance measure to monitor the activity "Expedite Material". Using a simple Time/Output Quantity chart, the Receiving Department C.I. Team tracks their improvements over the next three to six months.

Before the improvement plan was implemented, four to five expedites were performed each day. After the checklist was implemented, expedites dropped to 1 per day.

The chart, posted in their work area, indicates the Receiving Department C.I. Team chose the correct root cause and an effective action plan.

Activity Analysis and Activity Accounting Summary

Procurement Process

ACTIVITIES	TOTAL COST	VALUE	NON-VALUE	DEPARTMENT	OUTPUT QTY.	COST PER OUTPUT
Run MRP	$700,000	$700,000	$0	Planning	100	$7,000
Issue Requisition	$145,000	$145,000	$0	Planning	2,200	$66
Issue Purchase Order	$250,000	$250,000	$0	Purchasing	1,800	$139
Handle Vendor Problem	$140,000	$0	$140,000	Purchasing	450	$311
Expedite Purchase Order	$145,000	$0	$145,000	Purchasing	440	$330
Certify Vendor	$175,000	$175,000	$0	Purchasing	12	$14,583
Receive Material	$291,470	$291,470	$0	Receiving	2,500	$117
Move Material	$302,940	$0	$302,940	Receiving	11,000	$28
Expedite Material	$157,350	$0	$157,350	Receiving	1,250	$126
Inspect Material	$225,000	$0	$225,000	Quality	2,500	$90
Expedite Material	$80,000	$0	$80,000	Quality	500	$160
Reject Material	$90,000	$0	$90,000	Quality	400	$225
Certify Vendor	$185,000	$185,000	$0	Quality	15	$12,333
Return Goods to Vendor	$60,000	$0	$60,000	Quality	375	$160
Pay Vendor Invoice	$205,000	$205,000	$0	Accounting	1,500	$137
Contact Vendor	$72,000	$0	$72,000	Accounting	250	$288
Issue Debit Memo	$65,000	$0	$65,000	Accounting	375	$173
Store Material	$102,000	$0	$102,000	Warehouse	1,800	$57
Cycle Count Inventory	$40,150	$0	$40,150	Warehouse	2,500	$16
TOTAL COST	$3,430,910	$1,951,470	$1,479,440			
TOTAL PERCENT	100%	57%	43%			

Scenario

The Procurement's Process Manager has put together a C.I. Team consisting of a cross section of employees from Sales, Planning, Receiving, Quality, Accounting and the Warehouse. The Process Manager has requested the C.I. Team develop a plan to improve the productivity of the Procurement Process by 10% over the next six months.

Continued with Step 1: Identify Improvement Opportunities

	ACTUAL	BENCHMARK	OPTIMUM
Value Added	57%	90%	100%
Non-Value Added	43%	10%	0%

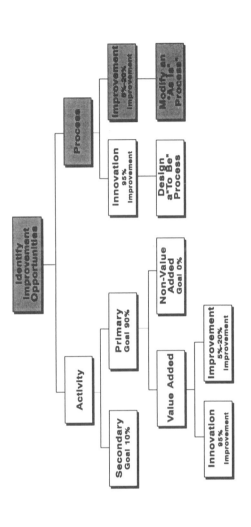

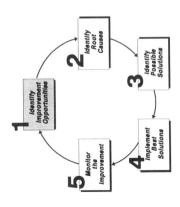

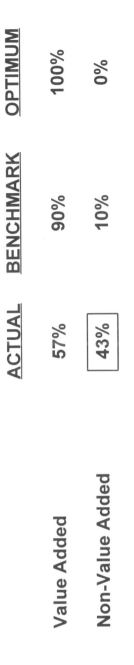

Using the ABM Activity Accounting Information for the Procurement Process, the C.I. Team recognized an extremely high Non-Value Added Cost Percentage. The Procurement C.I. Team, therefore, decided the greatest opportunity for improvement is likely reducing or eliminating several Non-Value Added Activities.

Continued with Step 1: Identify Improvement Opportunities

"As Is" Procurement Process

| Sales | Planning | Purchasing | Receiving | Quality | Accounting | Warehouse |

Diagram nodes:

- Sales: Do Sales Forecast, Take Customer Phone Order, Take Customer Mail Order
- Planning: Issue Requisition, Run MRP
- Purchasing: Handle Vendor Problems, Issue Purchase Order, Vendor, Expedite Purchase Order, Certify Vendor
- Receiving: Move Material, Receive Material, Expedite Material
- Quality: Expedite Material, Inspect Material, Reject Material, Return Goods to Vendor, Certify Vendor
- Accounting: Vendor, Pay Vendor Invoice, Contact Vendor, Issue Debit Memo, Vendor, Do Sales Forecast
- Warehouse: Manufacturing, Store Material, Cycle Count Inventory

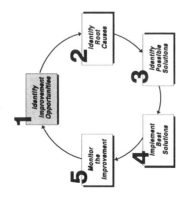

To improve the Procurement Process, the Procurement C.I. Team needs to visually understand the current "As Is" Process. Using basic flowcharting techniques, the C.I. Team mapped the existing Procurement Process by linking the Activity input(s) and output(s) using Post-it Notes on a piece of butcher paper on the wall.

Continuous improvement cycle:
1 — Identify Improvement Opportunities
2 — Identify Root Causes
3 — Identify Possible Solutions
4 — Implement Best Solutions
5 — Monitor the Improvement

Step 2: Identify Root Causes

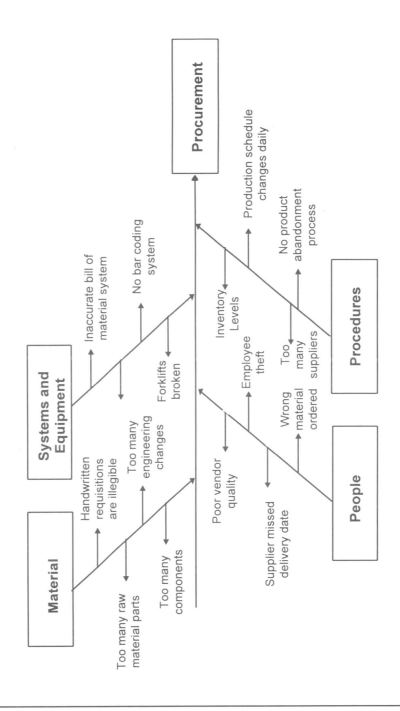

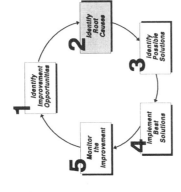

Using a Cause and Effect Diagram, the Procurement C.I. Team generated a list of "Root Causes" of the Procurement Process.

Continued with Step 2: Identify Root Causes

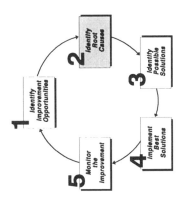

1 Identify Improvement Opportunities
2 Identify Root Cause
3 Identify Possible Solutions
4 Implement Best Solutions
5 Monitor the Improvement

Causes	Run MRP	Issue Requisition	Issue P.O.	Handle Vendor Problem	Expedite Purchase Order	Certify Vendor	Receive Material	Move Material	Expedite Material	Inspect Material	Expedite Material	Reject Material	Certify Vendor	Return Goods to Vendor	Pay Vendor Invoice	Contact Vendor	Issue Debit Memo	Store Material	Cycle Count Inventory	Total Root Cause Cost ($000's)
1. Supplier missed delivery date	✓		✓	✓	✓	✓		✓	✓		✓			✓		✓	✓			$1,022
2. Engineering Changes	✓	✓	✓	✓	✓	✓		✓	✓	✓	✓	✓	✓	✓	✓	✓	✓			$2,314
3. Poor vendor quality		✓	✓	✓	✓	✓	✓		✓	✓	✓	✓	✓	✓	✓	✓	✓	✓	✓	$3,430
4. Wrong material ordered	✓	✓	✓	✓	✓		✓		✓	✓	✓	✓	✓	✓	✓	✓	✓	✓		$2,095
5. Number of suppliers		✓	✓	✓		✓	✓			✓			✓		✓		✓			$1,553
6. Number of parts	✓	✓	✓	✓	✓	✓	✓		✓	✓	✓	✓		✓	✓		✓	✓	✓	$3,430
7. Daily production changes	✓	✓	✓		✓		✓		✓		✓			✓	✓	✓	✓			$2,633
8. Handwritten forms	✓	✓	✓	✓	✓				✓		✓						✓		✓	$2,268
9. Forklifts broken							✓	✓			✓							✓	✓	$933
10. Inaccurate bill of material	✓	✓	✓		✓		✓		✓	✓	✓	✓		✓	✓		✓	✓	✓	$2,890
Activity Cost ($000's)	$700	$145	$250	$40	$145	$175	$291	$303	$167	$225	$80	$90	$185	$60	$205	$72	$96.5	$102	$40	

Procurement Process Activities

Next, using a simple matrix, the Procurement C.I. Team selected and analyzed ten root causes and their affect on each of the Procurement Process Activities. If a Root Cause influenced an Activity's cost or volume, a check mark (✓) was placed in the matrix square. The total cost impact of each Root Cause was calculated by adding horizontally for each activity affected. For example, root cause number nine impacts five activities which collectively consume $933,400 costs.

The Analysis worksheet shows that root causes numbers three and five impact the most cost. The C.I. Team decides to focus on root cause #3, "Poor Vendor Quality of Incoming Raw Materials." Other root causes will be addressed later in the year.

Step 3: Identify Possible Solutions

Problem Statement

Define possible solutions to our poor quality of incoming raw material.

- Change vendors
- Develop vendor specifications
- Require vendors to perform 100% inspection
- Certify all vendors
- Charge a fee to vendors for items related to Poor Quality (Production downtime, etc.)
- Redesign products with fewer parts, requiring fewer vendors

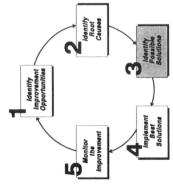

Using the C.I. technique of Brainstorming, the C.I. Team generated a list of possible solutions to reduce or eliminate poor quality of incoming raw material.

Step 4: Implement a C.I. Plan

Criteria	Weight	Certify Vendors	Redesign Product with Fewer Parts	Change Vendors	Require 100% Inspection
		Solutions			
Cost of Solution (How much will it cost to implement the solution?) — 10 = Low, 1 = High	30%				
Effectiveness of Solution (How effective would the solution be in addressing root causes and solving the problem?) — 10 = High, 1 = Low	30%				
Probability of Success (How likely is it that the solution itself could successfully be implemented?) — 10 = High, 1 = Low	20%				
Resistance (How much resistance might there be to implementing the solution?) — 10 = Low, 1 = High	10%				
Ease of Implementation (How easy would it be to implement the solution?) — 10 = High, 1 = Low	10%				
Total	100%				

Legend: Rating / Points (rating x weight)

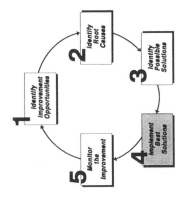

1 Identify Improvement Opportunities
2 Identify Root Causes
3 Identify Possible Solutions
4 Implement Best Solutions
5 Monitor the Improvement

After identifying a variety of solutions to "The poor quality of incoming raw material", the Procurement C.I. Team then proceeded to analyze what they felt were the four best solutions and then selected the best solution to implement. The Procurement C.I. Team used a decision matrix to analyze their choices. The criteria used to evaluate the possible solutions were: (1) cost, (2) effectiveness, (3) probability, (4) resistance, and (5) ease. The Procurement C.I. Team, working with their Process Manager, assigned a weight to each criteria. For example, cost was given a 30% factor.

Step 4: Implement a C.I. Plan

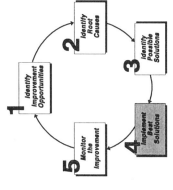

After rating each solution, the Procurement C.I. Team decided "Certifying Vendors" best met the needs for improving the Procurement Process.

Criteria	Weight	Solutions: Certify Vendors		Redesign Product with Fewer Parts		Change Vendors		Require 100% Inspection	
		Rating	Points	Rating	Points	Rating	Points	Rating	Points
Cost of Solution 10 = Low 1 = High (How much will it cost to implement the solution?)	30%	3	.9	2	.6	7	2.1	5	1.5
Effectiveness of Solution 10 = High 1 = Low (How effective would the solution be in addressing root causes and solving the problem?)	30%	8	2.4	7	2.1	6	1.8	1	.3
Probability of Success 10 = High 1 = Low (How likely is it that the solution itself could successfully be implemented?)	20%	9	1.8	6	1.2	2	.4	7	1.4
Resistance 10 = Low 1 = High (How much resistance might there be to implementing the solution?)	10%	6	.6	1	.1	5	.5	2	.2
Ease of Implementation 10 = High 1 = Low (How easy would it be to implement the solution?)	10%	6	.6	1	.1	5	.5	1	.1
Total	100%	6.3		4.1		5.3		3.5	

Key: Rating / Points (rating × weight)

Continued with Step 4: Implement a C.I. Plan

Estimate Impact of Plan

Procurement Process Activities	Before			After			Net Change	
	Output Quantity	Cost per Output	Total Cost	Output Quantity	Cost per Output	Total Cost	Output Quantity	Total Cost
Run MRP	100	$7,000	$700,000	52	$7,000	$364,000	-48	($336,000)
Issue Requisition	2,200	$66	$145,000	2,000	$66	$130,000	-200	($21,000)
Issue Purchase Order	1,800	$139	$250,000	1,600	$139	$222,400	-200	($27,600)
Handle Vendor Problem	450	$311	$140,000	200	$311	$62,200	-250	($77,800)
Expedite Purchase Order	440	$330	$145,000	200	$330	$66,000	-220	($79,000)
Certify Vendor	12	$14,583	$175,000	50	$14,583	$729,150	38	$554,150
Receive Material	2,500	$117	$291,470	1,600	$117	$187,200	-900	($104,270)
Move Material	11,000	$28	$302,940	8,000	$28	$224,000	-3,000	($78,940)
Expedite Material	1,250	$126	$157,350	500	$126	$63,000	-750	($94,350)
Inspect Material	2,500	$90	$225,000	0	$90	$0	-2,500	($225,000)
Expedite Material	500	$160	$80,000	200	$160	$32,000	-300	($48,000)
Reject Material	400	$225	$90,000	0	$225	$0	-400	($90,000)
Certify Vendor	15	$12,333	$185,000	50	$12,333	$616,650	35	$431,650
Return Goods to Vendor	375	$160	$60,000	100	$160	$16,000	-275	($44,000)
Pay Vendor Invoice	1,500	$137	$205,000	1,300	$137	$178,100	-200	($26,900)
Contact Vendor	250	$288	$72,000	50	$288	$14,400	-200	($57,600)
Issue Debit Memo	375	$173	$65,000	25	$173	$4,325	-350	($60,675)
Store Material	1,800	$57	$102,000	1,600	$57	$91,200	-200	($10,800)
Cycle Count Inventory	2,500	$16	$40,150	2,200	$16	$35,200	-300	($4,950)
Total Cost			$3,430,910			$3,035,825		($401,085)

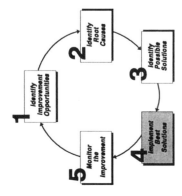

Before the Procurement C.I. Team developed their Action Plan, they estimated the impact of that Plan on all of the Procurement Activities. Each member of the team provided their best guess as to the impact of the improvement on the Activities their department performs. The next step to confirm reasonableness of this Plan was to create a revised resource plan for each Activity in each department.

Step 5: Monitor the Improvement

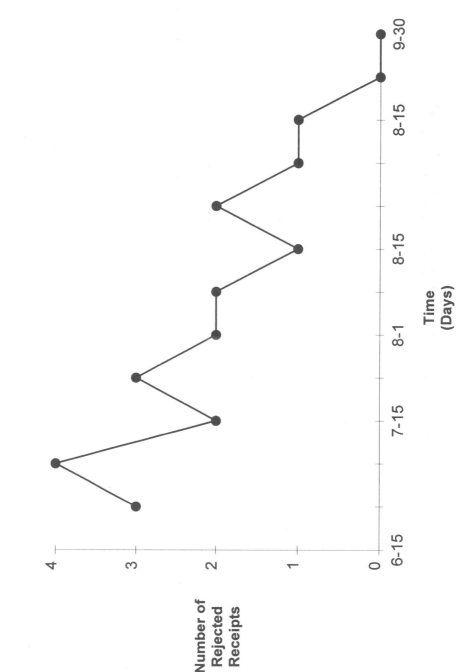

To monitor their improvement efforts, the Procurement C.I. Team developed a simple performance measure to monitor the quality of incoming raw materials. Using a simple Time/ Output Quantity chart, the Procurement C.I. Team could track their improvements over the next three to six months.

Activity Analysis and Activity Accounting Summary

Procurement Process

Scenario

The Procurement's Process Manager has put together a C.I. Team consisting of a cross section of employees from Sales, Planning, Receiving, Quality, Accounting and the Warehouse. The Process Manager has requested the C.I. Team develop a plan to innovate the Procurement Process.

ACTIVITIES	TOTAL COST	VALUE	NON-VALUE	DEPARTMENT	OUTPUT QTY.	COST PER OUTPUT
Run MRP	$700,000	$700,000	$0	Planning	100	$7,000
Issue Requisition	$145,000	$145,000	$0	Planning	2,200	$66
Issue Purchase Order	$250,000	$250,000	$0	Purchasing	1,800	$139
Handle Vendor Problem	$140,000	$0	$140,000	Purchasing	450	$311
Expedite Purchase Order	$145,000	$0	$145,000	Purchasing	440	$330
Certify Vendors	$175,000	$175,000	$0	Purchasing	12	$14,583
Receive Material	$291,470	$291,470	$0	Receiving	2,500	$117
Move Material	$302,940	$0	$302,940	Receiving	11,000	$28
Expedite Material	$157,350	$0	$157,350	Receiving	1,250	$126
Inspect Material	$225,000	$0	$225,000	Quality	2,500	$90
Expedite Material	$80,000	$0	$80,000	Quality	500	$160
Reject Material	$90,000	$0	$90,000	Quality	400	$225
Certify Vendor	$185,000	$185,000	$0	Quality	15	$12,333
Return Goods to Vendor	$60,000	$0	$60,000	Quality	375	$160
Pay Vendor Invoice	$205,000	$205,000	$0	Accounting	1,500	$137
Contact Vendor	$72,000	$0	$72,000	Accounting	250	$288
Issue Debit Memo	$65,000	$0	$65,000	Accounting	375	$173
Store Material	$102,000	$0	$102,000	Warehouse	1,800	$57
Cycle Count Inventory	$40,150	$0	$40,150	Warehouse	2,500	$16
TOTAL COST	$3,430,910	$1,951,470	$1,479,440			
TOTAL PERCENT	100%	57%	43%			

Continued with Step 1: Identify Innovation Opportunities

	ACTUAL	BENCHMARK
Value Added	57%	95%
Non-Value Added	43%	5%

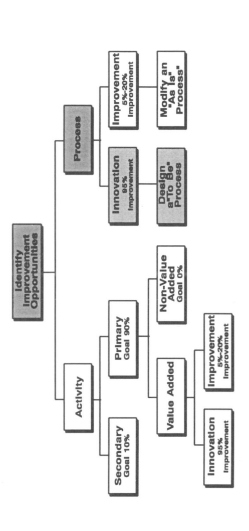

1 — Identify Improvement Opportunities
2 — Identify Root Causes
3 — Identify Possible Solutions
4 — Implement Best Solutions
5 — Monitor the Improvement

Using the ABM Activity Accounting Information for the Procurement Process, coupled with a benchmarking visit to an organization with a practice procurement system, the C.I. Team recognizes the greatest opportunity for improvement is to innovate their own process.

Appendix C

Continued with Step 1: Identify Improvement Opportunities

"As Is" Procurement Process

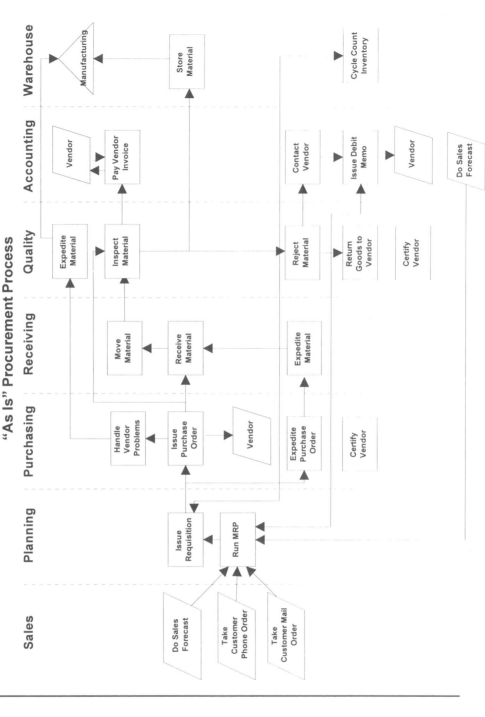

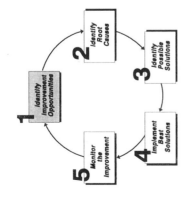

To innovate the Procurement Process, the Procurement C.I. Team needs to visually understand the current "As Is" Process. Using basic flowcharting techniques, the C.I. Team mapped the existing Procurement Process by linking the Activity input(s) and output(s) using Post-it Notes on a piece of butcher paper on the wall. The information was shared with the benchmarking partner.

The "As Is" process was then put aside. To effectively create a re-engineered "To Be" process requires starting with a blank sheet of paper. The team proceeded to the next step.

Continued with Step 1: Identify Innovation Opportunity

"To Be" Procurement Process

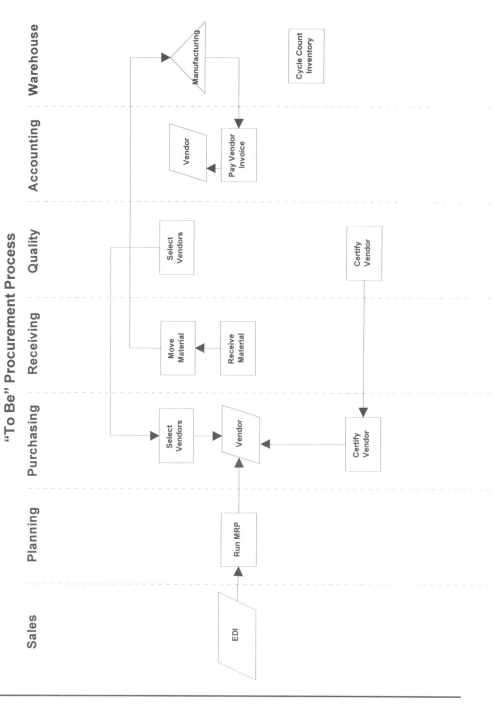

| Sales | Planning | Purchasing | Receiving | Quality | Accounting | Warehouse |

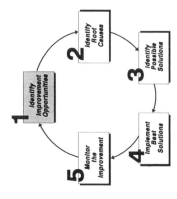

To innovate the Procurement Process, the Procurement C.I. Team designed a new "To Be" Process, utilizing insight and lessons learned from their benchmarking visit, coupled with common sense assumptions of what can work in their organization.

The process they designed requires:

1) Electronic transfer of sales orders instead of paperwork or phone calls;

2) No purchase orders. Vendors tap into the MRP system to schedule shipments;

3) Vendors are paid on what is used by manufacturing, not what is received.

Step 2: Identify Root Causes

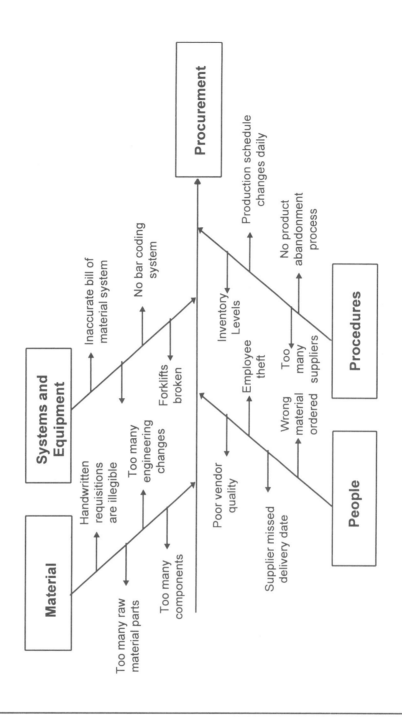

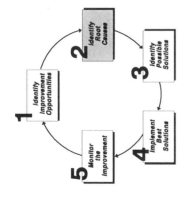

Using a Cause and Effect Diagram, the Procurement C.I. Team generated a list of all the causes related to the "As Is" Procurement Process. The causes must be addressed to achieve the "To Be" re-engineered process.

Step 3: Identify Possible Solutions

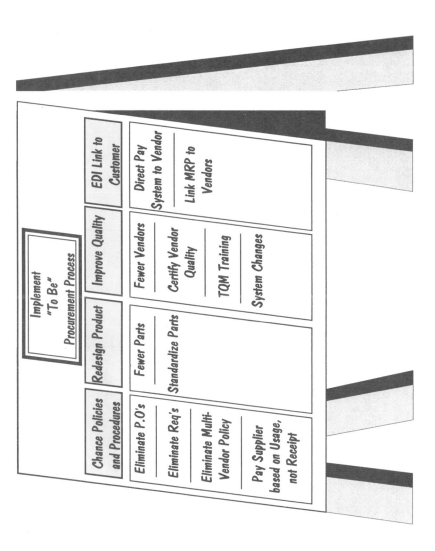

Implement "To Be" Procurement Process

Change Policies and Procedures	Redesign Product	Improve Quality	EDI Link to Customer
Eliminate P.O.'s	Fewer Parts	Fewer Vendors	Direct Pay System to Vendor
Eliminate Req's	Standardize Parts	Certify Vendor Quality	Link MRP to Vendors
Eliminate Multi-Vendor Policy		TQM Training	
Pay Supplier based on Usage, not Receipt		System Changes	

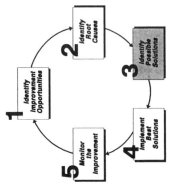

1 Identify Improvement Opportunities

2 Identify Root Causes

3 Identify Possible Solutions

4 Implement Best Solutions

5 Monitor the Improvement

Using the Storyboarding technique, the Procurement C.I. Team generated a list of possible solutions for achieving the ideal "To Be" Procurement Process.

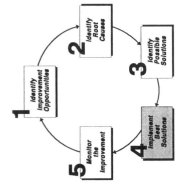

Continued with Step 4: Implement a C.I. Plan

Estimate Impact of Plan

Procurement Process Activities	Before			After			Net Change	
	Output Quantity	Cost per Output	Total Cost	Output Quantity	Cost per Output	Total Cost	Output Quantity	Total Cost
Run MRP	100	$7,000	$700,000	100	$7,000	$700,000	0	$0
Issue Requisition	2,200	$66	$145,000		N/A		-2,200	($145,000)
Issue Purchase Order	1,800	$139	$250,000		N/A		-1,800	($250,000)
Handle Vendor Problem	450	$311	$140,000		N/A		-450	($140,000)
Expedite Purchase Order	440	$330	$145,000	100	$330	$33,000	-340	($112,000)
Certify Vendor	12	$14,583	$175,000	20	$14,583	$291,660	8	$116,660
Receive Material	2,500	$117	$291,470	2,500	$117	$291,470	0	$0
Move Material	11,000	$28	$302,940	7000	$28	$196,000	-4,000	($106,940)
Expedite Material	1,250	$126	$157,350	600	$126	$75,600	-650	($81,750)
Inspect Material	2,500	$90	$225,000		N/A		-2,500	($225,000)
Expedite Material	500	$160	$80,000		N/A		-500	($80,000)
Reject Material	400	$225	$90,000		N/A		-400	($90,000)
Certify Vendor	15	$12,333	$185,000	15	$12,333	$185,000	0	$0
Return Goods to Vendor	375	$160	$60,000	100	$160	$16,000	-275	($44,000)
Pay Vendor Invoice	1,500	$137	$205,000	1,500	$137	$205,000	0	$0
Contact Vendor	250	$288	$72,000		N/A		-250	($72,000)
Issue Debit Memo	375	$173	$65,000		N/A		-375	($65,000)
Store Material	1,800	$57	$102,000		N/A		-1,800	($102,000)
Cycle Count Inventory	2,500	$16	$40,150	2,500	$16	$40,150	0	$0
Total Cost			$3,430,910			$2,033,880		($1,397,030)

Before the Procurement C.I. Team develops their action plan, they must estimate the impact of that plan on all of their procurement activities. The next step to confirm reasonableness is to create a revised resource plan for each activity in each department.

Step 5: Monitor the Improvement

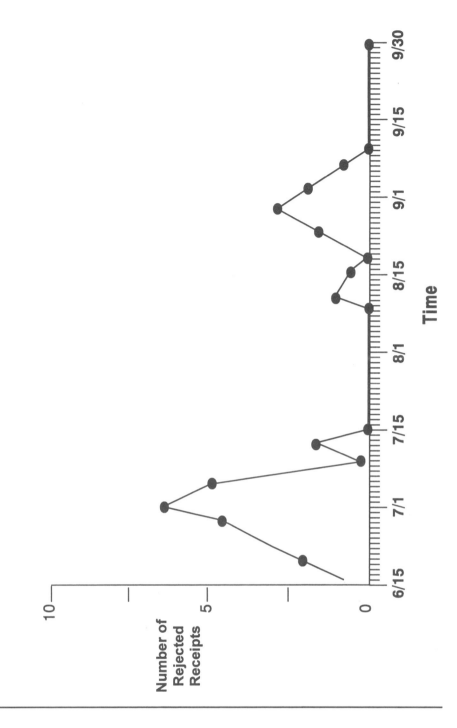

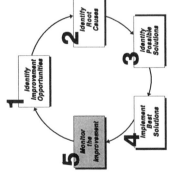

To monitor their improvement efforts, the Procurement C.I. Team developed a simple performance measure to monitor the quality of incoming raw materials. Using a simple Time/ Output Quantity chart, the Procurement C.I. Team could track their improvement over the next three to six months.

Index

A

ABM Coach
42, 43
ABM Hierarchy
13
Action Plans
122-23, 132, 152, 168-69, 181, 189
Activities
1, 8, 10, 13-14, 25, 29-30, 39, 41, 44, 52-53, 64, 70, 73, 79, 86, 91, 93, 105, 122-23, 127, 149-50, 162-63, 168-71, 175, 177, 181, 189
Activity
  Accounting
    1-2 13, 15, 20, 24-27, 30, 43, 49, 51, 159, 173-74, 183
    Interview
      25
    Definition of
      24
    Tips
      26
    Worksheet
      25, 27-28
  Analysis
    2, 20, 25, 27, 30, 49, 159, 173, 183
    Agenda
      20
    Interview
      13, 20-24
    Interview Questions
      21
    Worksheet
      24, 27
    Definition of
      23
  Based Budgeting (ABB)
    26, 40, 124, 127, 149, 156, 170
    Strengths of
      152-53
  Based Product Costing (ABC)
    1, 26, 149
  Based Management (ABM)
    1-2, 6-7, 10, 13, 16, 22, 26, 34, 36, 42, 51, 53, 55, 79, 111, 114, 131, 159, 161, 174
    Analysis
      53

(Activity Based Management Cont'd)
  Coach
    42-43
  Creating
    13, 20, 30
  Hierarchy
    13
  Team Exercise
    6
Characteristics
  18-19, 30
Cost per Output
  26, 81, 84, 132, 141-45, 151-53, 156, 160
Definition of
  15, 56-57
Dictionary (Sample Page)
  19
Improvement
  5, 36-38, 159
Innovation
  37
Non-Value Added
  4, 17-18, 20-21, 23-24, 27, 30, 35, 37-38, 55-61, 63, 71, 74, 80, 87, 89, 98, 146, 151-52, 159-61, 174
Performance Measures
  40, 129, 130-32, 146
Primary
  7, 18, 20-21, 23-24, 27, 30, 37, 63, 65-66, 89, 96
Secondary
  7, 18, 20-21, 23-24, 27, 30, 37, 63-66, 89, 152, 160
  (See also Administrative)
Significant
  15, 16
Value Added
  7, 18, 20-21, 23-24, 27, 30, 35, 37-38, 55-56, 59-61, 63, 74-75, 89, 133, 146, 160-61, 174
Administrative Activities
  7, 18, 21, 23, 37, 63, 65
  (See also Secondary)
Agendas for...
  Step 1: Identify Improvement Opportunities
    49
  Step 2: Identify Root Causes
    91

Index

(Agendas for... Cont'd)
    Step 3: Identify Possible Solutions
        103
    Step 4: Implement Best Solutions
        117
    Step 5: Monitor the Improvement
        127
Appendix Exercises
    A - 159
    B - 173
    C - 183
"As Is" Process
    70, 73-74, 175, 185, 187

B

Benchmarking
    5, 26, 38, 49, 51, 53, 75, 79, 80-82, 84-87,
    132, 184, 186
    Actuals
        86
    Best in Class
        83
    Competitor
        83
    Definition of
        79
    Helpful Hints
        87
    Internal
        82
    Partner
        82-84, 86-87
    Rules
        80
    Steps to
        80
Blatt, James
    82
Brainstorming
    40, 44, 75, 91, 95, 97, 100, 103, 105-8,
    111, 178
Business Process
    4, 7, 10, 13-14, 19-20, 30, 38, 53, 55-57,
    70-75, 79, 82, 84, 87, 89, 127, 132
    Analysis
        38, 49, 53, 71, 75
    "As Is"
        70, 73-74, 175, 185, 187
    Definition of
        14, 30, 69

(Business Process Cont'd)
    Improvement
        5, 36, 38, 73-74
    Innovation
        38, 74
    Maps
        26
    Performance Measures
        140
    Re-Engineering
        5, 74-75
    Steps to
        70
    "To Be"
        74-75, 185-188
    Typical List of
        72

C

Case Study
    (See Appendix)
Cause and Effect Diagramming
    39, 44, 53, 91, 93-94, 96, 100, 162-163,
    176, 187
    Analysis
        91
    Shortcut
        98
    Steps to
        94
    Tips
        95
    Worksheet
        97
Chartier, Emilie
    105
Continuous Improvement (C.I.)
    1-2, 5, 7-9, 20, 26, 33, 35-36, 38-45, 52,
    57, 63, 71, 74, 79, 85, 93, 95-96, 98, 100,
    105-107, 114, 119, 127, 129-132, 149, 165
    Committee
        41-43, 117, 127
    Five Steps to
        1, 26, 34, 53, 151, 159
    Leader
        41, 43-45, 112
    Meeting Rules of Etiquette
        45
    Pitfalls
        35

(Continuous Improvement Cont'd)
Plans
105, 117, 119, 125
Process
33-35, 132
Steps to
34
Team Meetings
2, 43
Teams
29, 35, 41, 111-113, 120-122, 124,
151, 159, 161-171, 173-182
Work Session
43-45
Chapter Summary
10, 30, 100, 125, 146, 156
Characteristics, Activity
19
Non-Value Added
4, 7, 18, 20-21, 23-24, 27, 30, 35,
37-38, 55-61, 63, 71, 74, 80, 87,
89, 98, 146, 151-52, 159-61, 174
Primary
7, 18, 20-21, 23-24, 27, 30, 37, 63
65-66, 89, 96
Secondary
7, 18, 20-21, 23-24, 27, 30, 37,
63-66, 89, 152, 160
(See also Administrative)
Value Added
7, 18, 20-21, 23-24, 27, 30, 35,
37-38, 55-56, 59-61, 74-75, 89,
133, 146, 160-61, 174
Cost Center
14, 16, 18, 20, 24, 63
Cost Per Output
26, 81, 132, 151-153, 156, 160

D

Decision Trees
36, 166-167, 179
Department
1-2, 13-16, 18, 20-24, 26-27, 29, 36, 38,
41, 49, 53, 55-57, 60, 63, 66, 70, 81-82,
85, 89, 97, 99, 108, 114, 123, 127, 150-51,
153, 168-69, 189
Mission Statement
22

Developing a Continuous Improvement Plan
119
Dewey, John
111
Dictionary, Activity (Sample Page)
19
Digital Equipment Corporation
82
Drucker, Peter E.
93

E

Edison Brothers Stores, Inc.
82
Excellence
1-2, 4-5, 7-8, 34-35, 39

F

Fishbone Diagram
93, 96-97, 100
Five Principles of Excellence
4-5, 10
Five Steps of...
Continuous Improvement
1, 26, 34, 53, 151, 159
Activity Based Budgeting
150
Business Process Analysis
70
Continuous Improvement
35
Storyboarding
112
Five Why's
53, 98-99, 164
Flowcharting
73, 185
Four Steps to
Benchmarking
80
Cause-and-Effect Diagramming
94
Implementing a C.I. Plan
120
Ford Motor Company
69
Function
13-14, 36, 38, 41, 82, 149

Index

G

Goal, The
129
Goldratt, Eli
129

H

Helpful Hints
61, 87, 114
Header Cards
113
Honda
4
How to use this book
i-ii

I

Improvement plan
127, 169, 171
Improvement Target Form
89
Inactivity
23
Indianapolis 500 Pit Crew (Roger Penske)
1, 83
Information Anxiety
36
Input
17, 19-21, 23-24, 27, 30, 70, 73, 175, 185
Internal benchmarking
87

J

Just-In-Time
5, 56

K

Kick in the Seat of the Pants, A
34

M

Mary Kay Cosmetics
83
Meeting Agendas
49, 91, 103, 117, 127

Motorola
1
Mutual Benefit Life
69

N

Non-Value Added
4, 7, 18, 20-21, 23-24, 27, 30, 35, 37-38, 55-61, 63, 71, 74, 80, 87, 89, 98, 146, 151-52, 159-61, 174
Non-Value Analysis
37

O

Organizational chart
14
Output
7, 10, 16-20, 22, 30, 39, 57, 70-71, 73, 85, 131-33, 153, 175, 185
Measure
17, 19, 21, 23-24, 26-27, 30, 80-81
Measure Guidelines
17
Measure Quantity
26, 150

P

Pareto
Analysis
39, 53, 96, 163
Chart
96
Penske, Roger (Indy 500 Pit Crew)
1
Performance Measure
7, 26, 52, 127, 129-32, 146, 171, 182, 190
Peters, Tom
7
Practice of Management, The
93
Primary
Activity
7, 18, 20-21, 23-24, 27, 30, 37, 63, 65-66, 89, 96
Analysis
18, 37-38, 49, 51, 53, 63

(Primary Cont'd)
    vs. Secondary Analysis
        18, 63, 64
    to Secondary Ratio
        35, 37
Process, Business
    4, 7, 10, 13-14, 19-20, 30, 38, 53, 55-57,
    70-75, 79, 82, 84, 87, 89, 127, 132
    Analysis
        38, 49, 53, 71, 75
    "As Is"
        70, 73-74, 175, 185, 187
    Definition of
        14, 30, 69
    Improvement
        5, 36, 38, 73-74
    Innovation
        38, 74
    Maps
        26
    Performance Measures
        140
    Re-Engineering
        5, 74-75
    Steps to
        70
    "To Be"
        74-75, 185-188
    Typical List of
        72
Procurement Map
    73
Product
    1, 4, 26, 56-57, 70, 84, 150

Q

Quality
    56-57, 70
Questionnaire
    8-9

R

Rate Your Readiness For Continuous
Improvement
    1, 8-9
Re-engineering
    74-75

Root Cause
    1, 35, 39, 49, 55, 58, 91, 93-94, 96-98,
    100, 103, 105-6, 112, 149, 162,-65, 171,
    177
    Analysis
        23, 26, 91, 93, 103
    Shortcut
        98
Rules for Benchmarking
    80

S

Secondary Activities
    7, 18, 20-21, 23-24, 27, 30, 37, 63-66, 89,
    152, 160
    (See also Administrative)
Secondary Analysis
    37
"Significant Activity"
    15-16
Solution Rating Matrix
    40, 120-21
Southwest Airlines
    1, 83
SPC Charts
    133-36, 141-44, 146
Steps to Continuous Improvement
    (See also Agendas)
    1: Identify Improvement Opportunities
        160-61, 174-75, 185
    2: Identify Root Causes
        91, 162-64, 176-77, 187
    3: Identify Possible Solutions
        103, 165, 178, 188
    4: Implement Best Solutions
        117
    5: Monitor the Improvement
        127, 170-71, 182, 190
Storyboarding
    40, 44. 103, 113-14, 165, 188
    Example
        113
    Helpful Hints
        114
Survey
    8-9

Index

T

Targets (Improvement Opportunities)
:   51
Task
:   13, 15, 19, 87
Task analysis
:   15, 38
Team Exercises
:   3, 6, 27-29, 56, 59-60, 65-66, 76, 86, 89, 97, 99, 108, 114, 124, 130, 155
    Explanation of
    :   1, 2
Texas Instruments Defense Systems
:   83
Thompson, Charles
:   107
Three Principles of Performance Measurement
:   131
Three Steps to Brainstorming
:   106
Time Percentage
:   20, 23-24, 27
Time/Output Quantity chart
:   171, 182, 190
Timeframe (Improvement Opportunities)
:   52
Tips
:   16, 26, 95
"To Be" Process
:   74-75, 185-88
Top 10 Strengths of Activity Based Budgeting
:   152-53
Top 10 Weaknesses of Traditional Budgeting
:   149
Total Quality Management
:   5, 26, 56
Traditional Budgeting
    Weaknesses of
    :   149
Traditional Management
:   2, 3, 10
Training (Improvement Opportunities)
:   53
Trend Charts
:   133-37, 139-43, 145-46

V

Value Added
:   7, 18, 20-21, 23-24, 27, 30, 35, 37-38, 55-56, 59-61, 63, 74-75, 89, 133, 146, 160-61, 174
Value Analysis
:   18, 26, 37-38, 49, 51, 53, 55
von Oech, Roger
:   34

W

Walmart
:   1
Waste
:   10, 55, 57-58, 80, 87, 152
Weekly C.I. Team Meetings
:   43
Wurman, Richard
:   36

X

Xerox
:   79